# SMALL-TREE GARDENS

*Simple Projects, Contemporary Designs*

# SMALL-TREE GARDENS

*Simple Projects, Contemporary Designs*

## HAZEL WHITE

*Photography by Matthew Plut*

CHRONICLE BOOKS
SAN FRANCISCO

Dedicated to Jackson Plut

Library of Congress
Cataloging-in-Publication Data:
White, Hazel.
Small-tree gardens : simple projects, contempo-
rary designs / Hazel White ; photography by
Matthew Plut.
p.   cm.
"A garden design book."
Includes bibliographical references.
ISBN 0-8118-2123-4 (pbk.)
1. Ornamental trees.  2. Gardens—Design.
I. Plut, Matthew.  II. Title
SB435.W418  2000
635.9'771—dc21                    99-17658
                                          CIP

Printed in Hong Kong.

Designed and typeset by David Bullen Design.

Distributed in Canada by Raincoast Books
8680 Cambie Street
Vancouver, British Columbia  V6P 6M9

10  9  8  7  6  5  4  3  2  1

Chronicle Books
85 Second Street
San Francisco, California 94105

www.chroniclebooks.com

# CONTENTS

# INTRODUCTION

Trees imprint a garden with wildness and permanence. Of all the elements we borrow from the natural landscape for our gardens, they are the largest. Even a small tree grows over our heads, its branches softening the sharp lines of the house walls or throwing flickering shadows over the path. Each growing season in the garden, for many decades, is recorded in its wood. The roots go deep and far into the earth, and the top—the realm of birds and breezes and untouched flowers—links the garden with the sky.

Beneath a wide-spreading tree lies a quiet sheltered space. During each gust of wind in the branches, light wobbles in the shade at your feet like underwater light, the show fading and sharpening as the sunshine comes and goes. In a lull, a leaf drifts down to the ground, rocking on its midrib until it's still. The view out into the garden appears deeper and prettier through the frame of the branches, and if the branches frame your house, it will look as if it's always been there, settled into the land and sanctioned by nature.

Two trees also create an interesting space. Planted one on either side of a gate or a porch, they mark the portals of the threshold between street and garden, or garden and house, and lend a sense as you pass through that you've arrived somewhere special. Groups of trees make private avenues to stroll in, your feet in crisscrossing shadows, your head under sheltering boughs; or an oasis enclosed behind scrims of leaves that obscure the deck next door and lift your eyes out over the top of it.

A garden with trees is sensuous: a mass of foliage rising into the sky contrasts beautifully with a simple flat lawn or gravel terrace and the delicate petals in the flower beds. Tree shadows play against sunlight in the open areas of the garden, creating a rich variety of experiences as you walk along a path into the shade under an overhanging tree. The cooler temperature quickly registers on your skin, and then you emerge into sunshine again, which feels more lovely because of the contrast.

We are phototropic creatures; we love light, especially the play of light. In the old farmhouse in England where I grew up, the windows were small to keep out the draughts and cold. A 100-foot Lombardy poplar marked the place where the driveway turned into the garden in front of the house. Its roots had created hills in the lawn and puckered the garden wall; its leaves shivered and whistled in a tall waterfall that turned yellow in autumn; and its shadow in the low angle of the sun stretched to the porch over the front door. Sitting there out of the wind on a cold day in spring, I'd wait sometimes twenty minutes at a time for the sunshine to break through the drifting clouds. Then I'd swing my legs in the tree shadows and pretend for a few silly moments that it was summer.

I've lived in California now for fifteen years, and sometimes I'd give a week's wages for a day of clouds and changing light. I miss shadows stealing across the West Country landscape, jumping hedges from field to field and riding over the villages to the south toward the English Channel.

A decade ago, with an unusual sense of urgency, I planted ten trees in my new urban garden on a hill in San Francisco. Surefootedly, and almost unconsciously, I turned a sunny house and south-facing garden, which had no privacy from any side, into an aerie in the treetops, where light sparkles through in glinting beams. Hot bright sunlight is visible from the house and deck, across the treetops and sweeping a terrace at the end of the garden where apples roll out from beneath a curtain of silver birch leaves. But close to the house, the light that streams through the silk trees is green and dappled; it plays over the deck, runs through the window shades, and makes peaceful patterns on the kitchen floor.

For a few glorious weeks in autumn, every tree leaf is pure yellow, and all I can see of the world is shivering gold and blue sky. In winter, most of the screening drops to the ground, and I look out into city streets, freeway, an old red brick factory chimney, and a silver streak of San Francisco Bay. I love the light then. I stand outdoors and stare at a neighbor's house bearing 25-foot gray patterns of my tree trunks and branches, while I listen to the split brown seedpods on the silk trees clicking in the cold wind. When it rains, the trees are reflected in the sheen of water on the deck, and beads of raindrops hang from the fine twigs of birch almost touching the path. When spring comes, the first sign will be a smear of green at the top of a birch tree that has scaled the surrounding houses and is the first touched by the sun.

No garden is too small for a tree. Most of the tree gardens in this book were designed for small places: an entrance garden, a side passage, alongside a garden shed or an arbor, at an intersection of garden paths or at the corner of a path. There are avenues of trees for small gardens and a dry creek bed with trees, as well as a maple woodland that could fill a pocket-handkerchief urban courtyard.

The gardens are all easy to build. The ones categorized as moderately difficult merely contain more steps than the others or require more attention to detail or a certain level of confidence. If you've never planted a tree before, don't be daunted; it's as easy as planting a rose bush, and most of the tree gardens in this book don't need pruning, or fertilizing, or spraying, or any kind of coddling at all.

Trees have special roles to play in decorating gardens and in making living spaces outdoors; the secrets of designing with trees are in the first chapter. The next chapter, "Simple Tree Gardening Skills," describes the practical business of choosing, planting, pruning, and caring for trees.

The tree garden "recipes," in the chapters that follow, contain all the information you need: lists of plants, tools, materials, and the how-to steps for creating each garden. The requirements of each tree are described—sun or shade, what kind of soil, and the USDA zones it thrives in. Most of the trees grow well in most gardens. But, if the tree doesn't match your situation, shop for a similar tree, one with the same design characteristics, for example, airy, wide-spreading, and spring blooming. An experienced person at your local nursery or a mail-order company will be delighted to help.

Even in the smallest garden, it's possible to make a place where you can feel you've taken to the woods. An upturned bucket behind a blossoming bough of your young apple tree or at the foot of your katsura tree when it's popping with yellow pollen one morning in spring is an invitation to withdraw from the world for a while, to touch wood and let your eyes drift up above it all, to the treetops and off into the wild sky.

# DESIGNING WITH TREES

Trees give a garden structure and decorate it. They make living walls and ceilings to enclose the garden from the street, the neighbors, or busier parts of the garden. Like architecture, they extend shelter over a piece of land and begin to make of it a definite place. But, unlike architecture, trees also move with the breeze, softening the light into dancing patterns of leaf and branch, produce flowers in almost infinite number over our heads, and change through the seasons, marking out years of beautiful days as they grow. This chapter explains the secrets of designing gardens with trees.

TREE ROOMS, SHELTER ⋘ At the Place des Vosges, in Paris, horse chestnut trees, three deep, their tops trimmed into box shapes, line each side of a small rectangular park. You know for certain that you have left the city behind as you pass into the darkness under the clipped arches and see ahead the sunlight sweeping the lawns and fountains. Here is a place of dalliance: men tug loose ties and roll up white shirtsleeves, women remove polished shoes and expensive stockings to bare their legs to the sun. Like the nude bathers lolling by the river in Cézanne's paintings, they are protected by the shelter of trees. At the center of the garden, the point farthest from civilization, five untrimmed horse chestnuts toss their foliage high in the sky. City children play games of imagination here on the dark floor, a roof of flickering foliage over their heads and a river of shadows around their knees.

You can make a separate space in your garden with one broad-spreading tree. The air is cooler under a tree's canopy, the light green and shadowy, the sounds of birdsong and leaf rustling against leaf become louder than the traffic, and the world withdraws far away. The space is more sheltering if the leafy ceiling is low; if the foliage drapes almost to the floor, as that of a weeping willow or mayten tree does, you have walls as well as a ceiling—in fact, an outdoor room open to the breezes and almost as secluded as a summerhouse.

Plant a series of trees around a garden, and the trunks form walls; leave the center clear so that it fills with sunlight and you have an open-air room like a woodland clearing. Or plant the garden almost solidly with trees, in a copse or orchard arrangement, and you make a large room with internal pillars and a vaulted ceiling.

Even if the trees have bare branches in winter, the sense of a room remains. Walking in over the threshold, between the portals of tree trunks, leaving the open garden behind, you pass into a different realm, "almost like leaving land to go into water, another medium, another dimension," writes John Fowles, in his essay "The Tree." "When I was younger, this sensation was acute. Slinking into trees was always slinking into heaven."

DAPPLED SHADE ⋘ Christopher Alexander, an architect and author of *A Pattern Language,* believes we orient ourselves toward places where light is "happening," where the light is exciting because it's not uniform. This is why the places we love and use the most, he says, "are places like window seats, verandahs, fireside corners, trellised arbors." We are usually happier in uneven light than in full sunshine. And more often we'll choose a bench under a tree where sunlight wobbles and plays around our feet and illuminates the view rather than an unsheltered spot under wide open sky.

For light shade, plant airy, graceful, open-branched trees. Silk trees, jacarandas, and locust trees have leaves composed of numerous leaflets along a main stalk or midrib, and every small leaflet flutters and lifts on a breeze. Their branches are relatively lightly clothed with foliage, so some light travels through in unbroken beams. A deck in the shelter of such trees will swim with cool filtered light through the summer and then, when the foliage is gone, be open to every ray of winter sunshine.

DEEP SHADE AND SUNSHINE ⋘ Beautiful gardens have a good balance of darkness and light. Landscape architect Ron Herman designed a garden so that one part of the client's house overlooks an expanse of open water; other rooms give onto an enclosed courtyard garden; and one part nestles into a redwood forest, the branches touching the eaves. It's cool on the side of the house under the trees. A stone lantern placed among the redwoods pulls the eye into the darkness, a soft diffuse primeval darkness, still and silent except for the occasional sighing of the treetops. The brown-black shade around the trunks of the trees is solid, though a streak of emerald-green light chances onto the forest floor sometimes, illuminating a patch of dampness that has dripped from the trees.

If you can arrange for light in one part of the garden and darkness in another—perhaps as simply as planting a tree to overhang a gate that leads into a sunny area—both areas will be enhanced by the contrast. Stopping to open the gate, you'll feel the change of temperature on your skin. If it's a dark-leafed tree, such as a purple-leafed plum, underplanted with black mondo grass, you'll feel the frisson of darkness more keenly and the return to the sunlight beyond the gate more pleasurably.

You can lead people into your garden and on a beautiful journey through it by arranging a sequence of sunlight and darkness. The balance of light to shade will depend on your climate, but, even in a cool, rainy climate, a varia-tion in light will greatly enhance the garden. Remember that we like to move toward light, so draw people forward through the garden by providing glimpses of light ahead. In a hot climate, the paths through the garden might be evergreen tunnels of shade opening onto a fountain sparkling in a patch of sunshine. In cool climates, a path might run along a sheltering but sun-dappled allée of trees with a view through to an open sunny lawn.

Don't be hesitant about creating shade. The greater the contrast in light levels, the clearer the definition of the different places in the garden and the richer the experience of the garden. There's just one mistake to avoid—plant-ing a tree with a large dense canopy in a small yard, which will black out the garden below. We dread living in such all-encompassing darkness. If you inherit a large, dark tree and can't find it in your heart to remove it, read the next section to see how one designer tricked the light into the shade.

### A BEAUTIFUL SHADE GARDEN ⋘ Garden designer Sharon Osmond moved into a house under a mature evergreen ash. Its limbs had grown high over the urban garden and far out over the neighbors' fences. Squir-rels ran along them, and the treetop rustled with robins, bushtits, towhees, and chickadees.

Wanting to screen the neighbors' decks and windows, on the garden boundaries she set about planting small trees—azaras, maples, a redbud, a weeping Kashmir cypress, and an acacia—which have grown to touch the lowest branches of the ash. Into this small garden with its green ceiling and green walls, slants of light come creeping across the brick paving yard by yard or down through layers of foliage in shifting spotlights. The garden glows with light gleaming against the shade.

Every few years, Sharon has a tree pruner thin the ash to reveal the structure of its old branches and to let the light stream through. The small trees, all airy, scrimlike species, nothing heavy or dense like a rhododendron, are also pruned regularly, to let the light, double-dappled now, steal on through to the garden floor.

Plants with shiny foliage—for example, azaras and Silver Sheen pittosporum—reflect light off their tiny-mirrored surfaces. In the deepest shade, close to the garden floor, splotches of paleness on the pulmonaria, coleus, and variegated ivy leaves, and the stripes on the variegated grasses read like dappled light.

In the thick of the garden plantings, where nicotianas vine up through a pieris and catch the lowest branches of a maple, sits a circle of light in a birdbath. Still water brings a picture of the bright sky down into many small water bowls distributed through the garden. As the overhead foliage moves, the water crinkles, and light glints off its surface.

Some areas of the garden have been made intentionally darker. In heavy shade at the side gate, under a cluster of maples below the ash, sits a black metal bench. Black pots with dark-green plants flank the bench, and in one is a black plastic spider. Passing through this area, you feel a shiver of melancholy, before stepping gladly back into the light.

Bowls of marbles and glass balls sit on the edge of the path, becoming whirlpools of brightness when the light streaks in low under the trees at sunset. The setting sun also warms a mannequin adorned with a necklace and splashes of blue paint; a reflection of her pleasure is posted on a full length mirror leaning against the garden shed.

BORROWING SCENERY, DRAWING VIEWS OUT ⋘ If you live in the country, you can borrow its scenery by planting in your garden a species of tree that is abundant in the local landscape. The eye will skip from your single tree, a slim pole of eucalyptus, for example, to its relatives over the fence and set bouncing your memories of the scents and wind and wildness in the surrounding woods.

The principle is the same for expanding the perception of space in urban gardens. Designer Suzanne Porter has planted a small dark-foliaged tree-shrub, a purple smokebush, close to her garden boundary, so that the eye travels from it to the tall purple-leafed plum in a neighbor's yard, and from there across the treetops in other neighbors' yards up into the sky. Without that visual pathway, the eye flits about tamely within the garden walls.

A journey out of a yard up to the treetops, from domed shrubs to round-crowned trees, or from purple to purple, this way, then that way, then up and up and up, reminds me of the escape of Baron Cosimo Piovasco di Rondo, from his ancestors' home to a life in the treetops (*The Baron in the Trees* by Italo Calvino). The first night, Cosimo stayed in the garden tree; then the touching branches of a neighboring tree beckoned, and he went off over the garden wall into the wide world and never came down to the ground again.

Scenery can also be borrowed by mimicking a line or an arrangement of elements outside the garden. In wine country, the pattern of the vineyards might be repeated in an orchard inside the garden fence. In a roof garden in Manhattan, the silhouette of a trimmed juniper might borrow the spire on a skyscraper.

Sometimes the view is too awesome to want to bring all of it into the garden. Landscape architect Thomas Church built a pool and deck, and a glass-sided cabana with a fireplace, on the crest of a hill in northern California overlooking a thirty-mile view of salt marshes and mountains (the house sits lower on the slope). Native live oaks protect the pool area from wind; they also divide the view into segments, or panels. One branch stretches horizontally over the meandering silver streak of river, another arches in line with the mountain ridge in the far distance. Writing about the garden, in his book *Gardens Are for People,* Church explained that a view framed by tree branches gains depth and perspective.

FRAMING, DRAWING VIEWS IN ❧❧❧ In England, the entrances to churchyards are often marked by two yews, one on either side of the gate. Arriving, one sees the church door at the end of the path framed by the dark foliage. Sometimes the view is further tunneled by a porch over the gate, which cuts off the church steeple and sky. Passing over the threshold—through the frame, so to speak—one begins to fall into quietness and contemplation.

At a house entrance, you can choreograph a feeling that your guests have arrived somewhere special by placing two columnar trees, like sentinels, on either side of the door. For a greater effect, build up the frame by installing an awning over the door or placing a pair of potted trees on the path.

A bough of flowering cherry arching over the house makes an informal, romantic frame. Its blossoms, leaves, and shadows soften the architectural lines and settle the house into its surroundings much more effectively than drab shrubs planted around the house foundation.

If there's a mature tree on the driveway, consider whether pruning would produce a branch to frame the house. Landscape architects often want to reroute the driveway if there's an opportunity for the first view of the house to be through an old oak.

Consider framing features within the garden, such as a bench or a potting shed, with a pair of trees or arching branches. At the Bloedel Reserve in Washington, the canopy of a large maple frames a dwarf maple with intricate twisted branches and finely cut foliage (see page 2).

A PLACE IN THE TREETOPS ❮❮❮ I love the drawings in landscape architecture books showing houses on steep ground with decks cantilevered out, on stilts, over the slope into the treetops. In the photographs, you see cushions, large and comfortable enough to sleep on, among the mossy trunks coming up through cutouts in the deck. To my mind, this is the perfect form of outdoor living, to be levitated off the ground into an aerie, touching the treetops, halfway to the clouds.

If you have a deck off the house even 10 feet above the ground, you can create a tree house effect by planting trees below. Choose a broad-canopied tree, so that the branches will come in over the deck rail, and one that will grow to the right height, not so tall that the foliage is all high overhead. Silk trees are sensational for such a planting, because they bloom in waves across their tops, so that all summer you are looking over troughs of pink flowers and out to the sky.

If you have a mature tree at the far end of the garden, consider building a small deck there, about 8 feet or so off the ground, right under the canopy or

wrapping the trunk. It's exciting to climb a staircase to an outlook in a tree. The house and the garden you've just walked through look different from here. Maybe there's a squint of a view out over the city from this height or into a neighbor's trees.

SHADOWS ON THE WALL ⊰⊰⊰ Most gardens are richly decorated with flowers, myriad leaf and foliage shapes, walls, paving, and furniture. At best, variety makes an exciting garden. But, if you want to move someone to quietness and rest, consider a decoration as soothing as shadows of trees cast onto a wall. In winter, the shadows mark bright days from dull ones. During changeable weather, when the sky swells with light and then darkens, they sharpen and fade across the wall as you watch.

For the most elegant shadows, look for deciduous trees with a naturally fine branching structure, such as maples, deciduous magnolias, beeches, and birches. Two trees with magnificent structure, light and airy honey locust and heavy, knobby, pollarded London plane, lose their leaves early in fall and leaf out late in spring, so they are superb candidates for a shadow garden. Actually, any tree is beautiful when you come upon the structure of its top spread out on the garden floor.

Consider also the full black shadows that conifers make. A coned yew or pencil-thin Italian cypress has a replica of its geometry turning on the ground during each hour from sunrise to sunset. The shadow stretches long at each end of the day, huddles near the trunk at noon. Striking patterns can be made. Italian cypress or trimmed yew columns planted either side of a stone walkway in rows running north-south will throw bars of solid black shadow across the sun-splashed stone.

REFLECTIONS ON WATER ⊰⊰⊰ At Jack Chandler's garden in Napa Valley, a large pond catches the fall colors of the canyon trees. So as not to overwhelm the rest of the garden, the pond is hidden inside a ring of cattails and visible from only two places: inside the house and at an overlook on the water's edge. From the overlook, in the shelter of a tree, you see the house spread out peacefully in reflection, in a pillow of billowing yellow, red, and green trees.

In small gardens, plant a tree close to a pond if you have one, and train a branch or two out over the water. (Plant only the very tidiest trees near swimming pools, because of the litter.) Or place a tub or bucket of water under a tree. Walking by, head down, people will come upon a stunning tree detail up close—a floating willow leaf, lean as a crescent moon, or a reflection of a thick mossy apple branch making a black elbow against a twilight sky.

TREE ORNAMENTS ⋘ A birdhouse or blue bottles in the treetop draw the eye up into the branches and the life among the leaves. Sculptures of woodland spirits under the tree stir imaginings of the feel of the wind on one's cheek, the fragrance in the damp tunnels under the ferns, the cold silence of the garden in moonlight. A bell with a simple earthen sound like wood on stone calls the mind back to the present moment under this tree, to a breeze stirring on this wet winter morning, to a catkin glistening against drenched bark as the sun shines through.

Fallen branches make seats or bird tables or steps in a woodland path. Glass bottle-stoppers studded into the bark of a fallen tree left in place call attention to the scraggy mosses and mushrooming lichens still growing there. Stilts propping split branches can also be ornamental, displaying for view the tree's age, the sinew in its trunk, its tenacity against the elements. In Prince Charles's garden at Highgrove, England, in the shade of tall trees, gigantic old roots, tree stumps, and trunks form the walls of a sheltered hosta garden, called "the stumpery."

LEAVES ⋘ After a night storm, a path or a water bowl becomes a collection plate for leaves from around the neighborhood. A razor-edged green mulberry leaf and a smooth flat scythe of green-gray willow are absorbing the damp already, while a crinkled old brown boat-shaped leaf from a bigleaf magnolia rocks on its midrib and will blow about the garden for months before it starts to rot. Only occasional beech or hornbeam leaves turn up in an autumn medley; mostly, they hold firm to the trees well into winter, rattling in the wind unless their dry russet surfaces are pinned still by dollops of snow.

Motion is an exciting quality in a garden. Leaves on long leafstalks, such as katsura, birch, and redbud leaves, flutter and shiver in the wind. Little-leaf linden, a pyramid of dark-green foliage on a calm day, turns two-toned in the wind, its leaf undersides flickering silver among the green. On hot summer days, the motion is refreshing.

In many tree species, the color of the leaves when they burst out of the leaf buds in spring is different from their mature color. New growth might be pale apple-green, like new birch leaves. Some maples and eucalyptuses have reddish new growth; purple-leaf acacia bursts open in lavender. Evergreen conifers put on fuzzy soft extensions of light-green new growth in spring. You can draw attention to these moments by planting white woodland anemones with green veins on their petals under the conifer's two greens, for example, or red tulips to match the red in the new leaf bracts of an overhanging elm.

Mature leaves come in many colors of green, gray, purple, and gold. Some are also variegated, with cream margins or pinkish centers. Walking the lines of trees at a garden center, it's hard not to choose a range; if you have space for six small trees, why not have one purple-leafed species, one glaucous, one gold, and so on. The reason is the impossibility of integrating them into the garden. Variety usually makes "a restless, unfulfilled effect," writes Hugh Johnson, in *The Principles of Gardens*, "a furniture showroom, not a furnished room."

A tree with purple or gold or variegated foliage must be considered a large, strong ornament in a garden. If you plant one in an open view that contains flower beds and other colorful ornamentation, it could cause visual chaos. In such a location, you'll find it easier to work with a green-leafed tree with a decorative leaf pattern or one with a weeping form or a shiny leaf. Artists can pull off exciting effects with strong color; the rest of us, because trees are such a permanent installation in the garden, might better try for a more peaceful, simple effect in the treetops, at least in the main areas of the garden, or play with the temporary effects of fall leaf color.

FALL COLOR ⋘ Fall color can strike a tree like fire, the cold catching its exposed side and burning the green chlorophyll right up that flank. Once the chlorophyll in each leaf goes, the underlying colorful pigments begin to show. On some trees, each leaf turns color in its own time: this parrotia leaf is alight with red-orange on one edge, but the chlorophyll is still alive and green on the opposite edge, and there's a yellow spot in the middle; a sister leaf on the same twig is uniformly red already; and the lower leaves, closer to the trunk and sheltered, are still plain green. Or fall color can suffuse a tree. Dogwood leaves flush with rosy pinkness as the weather turns. And the leaves curl, showing their pale-pink undersides.

American yellowwood loses its fresh yellow fall foliage leaflet by leaflet. The large terminal leaflets hold on until last, and then, when they drop, the yellow leaf stalks remain for a while at the tips of the gray branches.

In the wild landscape, brown stalks, duff seedheads, and all the soft bruised colors of rot are the natural companions to fall color in the trees. I love to see gardens left alone in fall, seedheads of perennials knocking hollow against broken grass stalks, mildew spreading over lushly decaying leaves caught by the frost. Hostas, in particular, are excellently messy in fall.

To play up the subtle beauties of the trees turning color, avoid placing within the same view plants with showy berries or fall flowers that clash with the tree leaf color. Perhaps any flowers, other than obvious heralds of winter, such as asters and Michaelmas daisies, ruin the atmosphere of the season winding down into sleep. A backdrop of dark-green hedges or evergreen trees shows off fall color particularly well.

QUIET EVERGREEN BACKGROUNDS ⋘ Designers and landscape architects use most trees to create quiet green backdrops to, or frames for, the ornamental features of the garden. A solid plane of black-green yew exquisitely sets off a Washington thorn thick with scarlet berries. The principle is that one plant provides the quiet background against which the other stands out very clearly. A background of holly would be just as solid as yew but less quiet, because the leaves are spiny and shiny and the berries ornamental.

At first, it's hard to pass by the showy flowering trees at the nursery and pick out the more practical, plain green trees such as hornbeam and yew. Before you make a terrible mistake and buy only flowering trees, consider this, from Dame Sylvia Crowe's book *Garden Design:* "Planting may be either part of the structure of a garden or its interior decoration. Its structural role is by far the more important, just as the walls of a house, both for the protection they give and for their visual proportion are more important than the wallpaper."

As you build your garden, purchase the right ratio of walls to wallpaper. And once you've mastered the restraint necessary to pass by exotic flowering trees, except for the occasional ornament or focal point, try to restrain yourself again and make your walls homogeneous—all the same species or two or

three species with the same shade of green leaves. If you can do it, you'll be on your way to building a garden with a distinctive sense of place. Consider the special beauty of an old orchard planted with one kind of fruit tree, the feeling of unity, the charm. As you edit your wish list toward greater and greater simplicity, console yourself with the knowledge that miscellany, especially in the treetops, has absolutely no charm.

CONIFERS ⋘ In large gardens, conifers can make fine garden walls and backdrops to ornamental plantings. In small gardens, though, the effect of a number of mature conifers is usually too imposing.

Conifers have superb design characteristics. Their unchanging solid shapes convey a sense of stillness and calm to a garden. When deciduous trees lose their foliage and the ground is a flurry of wind-driven leaves, they stand like unruffled sentinels, their dark boughs sometimes decorated by silver hoar frost or a cap of snow. Cedar of Lebanon—very slow growing but eventually too large for small gardens—makes a year-round majestic silhouette with strong horizontal beams of branches that barely sway in a strong wind. Back-lit, the tree is pure line against the sky.

In a small garden, a somewhat dwarf columnar species, such as Skyrocket juniper, establishes a visual anchor in a planting of loose airy flowers; it's a stable green place for the eye to rest, and the neat matte green foliage provides a perfect foil for blowsy flowers. In a flat garden, a clipped and wired tower of Irish yew or two exclamation points of Italian cypress provide height. A container is the appropriate place in a small garden for a majestic conifer such as Japanese black pine; it's easily pruned to a giant bonsai.

BRANCHES ⋘ Saucer magnolias have smooth sinuous branches; in contrast, old apple branches may be all stout, rugged elbows and deep crevices where moss and mistletoe have taken hold. Some trees are twiggy; their winter outlines are thickets rather than graceful tracery against the sky. The branches of Hollywood juniper twist from the trunk at sharp irregular angles; the tree outline looks like flickering flames. If branches are long and soft, the wind will flip them about in constant motion during a storm; the sound can be distressingly loud and relentless to some people, thrilling to others.

Trees with strongly horizontal branching habits offer shelter under their canopies and a view out to the garden all around. Trees with weeping branches offer more enclosure; pyramidal or vase-shaped trees, less. Fastigiate or columnar cultivars have a strongly upright branching habit, providing very little shelter but making excellent vertical accents and screens.

BARK ❮❮❮ In a garden near Portland, Oregon, bark that shines like gold glass, on the trunks of Manchurian cherry trees, lights the understory at the edge of the woods and draws you along the narrowing path, under the ceremonious wooden arches, and down the wild hillside (see page 84).

Another cherry, the birch bark cherry, has mahogany-red bark that glistens in the sun. The bark of jacquemontii birch is silky white-cream and pink. Red ironbark is corrugated black with red furrows. Maple barks range from green with white diamond markings to peeling cinnamon brown to pink-gray. No bark is ordinary. Even if it's gray-brown, it may gleam in the rain, or fissure with age, or carry patterns of raised stitches or knotty tweed, or peel off in thin sheets or mottled plates.

The tree's bark might be what everyone sees first if the tree is at the edge of a path or near the house entrance. In those situations, and in avenues and geometric groves where the trunks form a strong rhythmic pattern, pay special attention to the characteristics of the bark. Its color may make the garden gorgeous in winter—imagine a grove of jacquemontii birch in the snow, the shiny wet white trunks splaying out from sparkling ice-crusted holes, the shadows of the lacy branches dancing over the field of snow.

FLOWERS ❮❮❮ A treetop of yellow laburnum blossoms on a gunmetal-gray day is pure ornament. The flowers descend from the dark wet branches in dangles as sweet as lemon curd and painted toys. The sight of them swinging in the breeze among lime green leaflets is enough to pull you out of the house into the elements, carefree without coat or umbrella into the wet grass and splattering raindrops.

Blossom on such a large scale—over our heads, into the sky—is heady while it lasts. When the season moves on, the petals drift down onto the garden floor, where it's good to have paving or a closely knit ground cover to catch and display them. It's then you notice that the apple blossom is streaked with purple veins, the dogwood blossom with green.

Tree blossoms stand out well against plain dark-green backgrounds. Construct such a setting by growing a dark-green creeper over a literal wall or by planting a wall of green trees (see page 20). Consider the character of the tree when it's out of flower, whether leaves, bark, and branching structure are worthy of a prime position alongside a path or shading a patio.

BERRIES ⋘ Berries weighing down tree branches establish a good reason to walk the garden in fall. When the loose clusters hang still, the air feels utterly quiet. A raindrop on one berry mirrors the other berries; the powdery bloom is smudged where the berries have rocked against one another in the wind.

Holly berries will draw the eye across the lawn and the fading flower beds to the edge of the garden, so striking is the effect of shiny bright berries studded tight along the branches among shiny dark-green leaves. Equally striking, and more unusual, are aralia's purple berries among its yellow fall leaves. For weeks, the light, tropical-looking canopy will bounce with birds feasting on the fruit.

SEEDS AND SEEDPODS ⋘ Seeds are as mesmerizing as ribbons or buttons. The sweetshade tree is festooned for months with clusters of black seeds, each in its crackly, brown, half-open seed case. Some appear alongside the last flush of butter-yellow summer flowers.

Some winged maple seeds are dainty red mobiles ('Osakazuki' Japanese maple), others chunky chains (red stripebark maple) ripening to the red of the fall leaves and leaf stalks. Many of the trees in the Leguminosae family produce their seeds in pods. About the time the autumn rains begin, the dry pods split, so that the seeds can fall into damp ground, but the empty pods hang on for a while, knocking against one another and the branches when the wind blows.

PLANTINGS UNDER TREES ⋘ If your tree has strong horizontal branching, you might consider planting nothing under it, and let the tree litter form its own ground cover. When you walk by, eyes down, the collection of fruits, leaves, and twigs spread out on the floor will remind you of the tree's nature and the passage of time—acorns and crumbling cinnamon leaves from last winter under a fresh herd of twigs from last week's gale. With nothing below the tree but natural litter, the view stays clear under an arching branch; and there's space to walk under the tree, stand there out of the wind or rain or heat, and look up into the canopy and out through it.

Moss is reminiscent of ancient forest floors. It mounds over every tree root and fallen branch, and its diminutive scale under soaring trees makes a majestic composition. It's a high-maintenance ground cover, however; patches die quickly if tree litter is left on the surface. In dry climates, it's impractical, because it needs too much care—weeding, watering, and feeding, plus the raking—so it's better to plant diminutive blue star creeper or baby's tears instead. Lawn grasses do poorly under spreading trees, because of the shade and the root competition. If you are planting trees in an existing lawn, consider cutting a neat circle out of the lawn around the tree trunks and leaving it bare. Rake the leaves so that the grass doesn't die beneath them.

Paving can be beautiful under trees, and it is especially appropriate if the tree will not tolerate regular watering (the paving should be open enough to allow some water to reach the tree roots). Gold or scarlet leaves may skitter over the paving in fall. Shadows play beautifully across the smooth surfaces of stone or concrete or decking, and sweeping up the litter is easy. Consider bark if the tree fruits stain.

SCREENS ⋘ For a garden to function as a garden, as a place of relaxation and connection to the natural world, it must provide privacy. We need to be able to amble about outdoors, following our whims, doing things our way, singing to ourselves, rediscovering the pleasures of solitude. So, most of us with urban and suburban gardens need screens.

The usual solution is to plant fast-growing "screening trees" that branch from the floor to the roof, that have dense foliage to make the screen solid, and of course that are evergreen, so the privacy is year-round. Be very careful about planting screening trees. They are almost always the culprits when a garden is overgrown, ugly, and dark. If you place trees around the boundary, right away the garden shrinks into itself, and you've only emphasized the smallness of the place.

Resolve from the beginning of your planning not to plant trees too large or dense for your garden; you don't want to barricade yourself in behind looming dark walls even if they are living ones. Then study just how little needs to be done to give your garden a strong sense of privacy. Think scrim instead of screen. Notice how airy trees that let sunlight through serve well enough to draw your eye away from what's behind them. Play with the idea of distracting attention from undesirable views, either by establishing bold focal points that hold the eye inside the garden or by providing escape routes out over the tops of them into the sky (see page 16).

QUICK RESULTS ⋘ Everyone who's grown trees will tell you not to choose trees on the basis of their speed of growth. They grow fast enough in the end, and it's a joy to watch them grow. Fast-growing trees are often short-lived or weedy looking. And if they outgrow their places you'll spend all your gardening hours lopping, sawing, and carting away foliage and branches by the truckload. While you wait for the tree of your choice to grow large enough to shelter you below it, set up an awning or an umbrella for privacy or block a horrid view with a fast-growing vine on a trellis in a pot.

Keep in mind what the late garden designer and writer Russell Page wrote in 1962 about planting for quick results: "One of the difficulties of gardening in our day comes, like many other problems, from the reckless speed we have imposed on ourselves. There is time only for the ready-made. . . . I myself feel gardening as a process and a garden at any stage on any day of the year is a whole world full of interesting things."

# SIMPLE TREE GARDENING SKILLS

It's natural for trees to grow—to flower and seed, and to grow new roots, new leaves, and new branches, and even to fight off the effects of pests and diseases and recover from gales and frosts. The magic is theirs; it's life. So don't think you have to become a horticulturist before you add a tree to your garden. In fact, planting trees has never been easier. Experts now agree that it's best to plant trees with a minimum of hoopla: no soil improvements, no stakes except in rare instances, no fertilizers, no fancy planting holes, no special pruning.

The preparation you need is rather to be a fussy shopper with a clear mission. The tree is going to provide beautiful structure to your garden for years to come. If you're following a recipe in this book, check that the tree listed is suitable for your climate and soil. Most of the trees will grow in most soils and most climate zones, but if a tree isn't suitable for you, don't lose sight of the design characteristics—you're looking not for any kind of tree for your alkaline soil but for one with a round crown that will soften the rooflines and produce dappled shade over the deck. A perfect tree exists. The search through the lexicon of tree shapes, leaf shapes, bark colors, flowers, fruits, and seeds is fun.

HARDINESS ZONES AND CLIMATE ⋘ Most trees will thrive in your garden unless your winters are very cold or your summers very hot. It's miserable to watch trees you've planted suffer in weather too extreme for them, so, before you buy, check which USDA zone you are in (your local nursery or county cooperative extension office will know, and catalogs from mail-order sources usually include a map of the USDA zones). Look only at trees that thrive in your zone. Then, to become completely confident that you're off to an uncompromised start with the absolutely right tree, read the following sections on wind and drought, sun and shade, and soil.

WIND AND DROUGHT ⋘ Trees have different degrees of wind tolerance. If you are planning to plant a tree in a windy place, plant one that is described as tolerating wind, to avoid a wide range of damage, from desiccated brown leaves and poor growth to snapped treetops and split trunks.

Although tree roots travel up to three times farther afield than their leaf canopies and are less susceptible to dry periods than roots of shrubs and perennials, most trees need moisture in the top 2 feet of the soil. In droughty climates, choose drought-tolerant trees, but remember to water them regularly for the first few years, until they are established.

SUN OR SHADE ⋘ In the main, trees grow best in full sun, out of the day-long shadows of tall buildings or larger trees. Flowering trees produce more flowers in full sun, and trees with fall color turn brighter colors if they are growing in sunshine. However, there are trees that thrive in partial shade, mostly trees that in their native habitat grow in the understory on the edges of woods, such as dogwoods, serviceberries, redbuds, and maples. During your selection process, check how well a tree tolerates shade.

IS YOUR SOIL RIGHT? ⋘ Most trees will thrive in a wide range of garden soils. Unless you have unusual conditions or choose a tree that's persnickety about something, your selection doesn't need to be matched to a soil analysis.

Drainage matters most. If you've seen water flooding in the area where you're planning to plant trees, don't choose a tree that is described as needing good drainage. If your soil is very sticky and heavy after rain, it probably has a high clay content and doesn't drain well.

Some trees prefer a good garden soil that contains organic matter and is always at least a little moist. Others prefer poor soil or die in regularly watered lawn. You probably already know whether your soil is deep and rich, easy to work, and easy to grow all kinds of plants in. Poor soil is too heavy to dig most of the year, or is full of fissures and gullies, or is so light that it's mostly sand and gravel, or is shallow over solid rock and doesn't hold enough water to sustain plants well.

IMPROVING YOUR SOIL ⋘ If you were planting vegetable seeds or perennials, it would make sense to improve your soil with organic matter, such as compost or aged manure or bark products. These amendments increase the soil's capacity to hold water and to drain well. But improving the soil over an area the size of a mature tree's root system is impractical—you'd need to go at least 2 feet deep and two or three times wider than the width of the mature leaf canopy. Even then, unless you replaced the entire block of soil, the fixing wouldn't work forever; you'd have to keep at it—without disturbing the growing roots. Best not to try, unless you're choosing a very small tree. Instead find a tree that grows in poor soil, and watch it flourish all by itself.

It's not recommended either that you try to fix your soil's pH (acidity or alkalinity) to make it more suitable for a particular tree. It rarely works unless you're prepared to do extensive work and keep doing it. Some books suggest adding amendments (lime to increase alkalinity, sulfur or acid mixes to increase acidity) to the soil you put back into the planting hole. That will help the new tree start out well, but in two or three or five years—the longer it is, the worse you'll feel—the roots will grow into the unimproved ambient soil, and, if that soil is poorly suited to the tree, you'll see it affect the tree's growth.

Simple soil pH kits are available from your local nursery. While you're there, you might ask about the soils in your area; an experienced nursery professional will know much more than you'll glean from your test. And if you look in the trees section of the nursery, you'll find the selection that has proved reliable in local gardens. From there, you can become more sophisticated if you're enjoying the search. Call specialist nurseries and describe which common trees thrive locally; they'll know which rarer ones will suit your garden well.

RED-FLAG WORDS ⋘ Many trees that are *fast growing,* words that cause gardening hearts to leap, are also described as *weedy.* In your fervor to have a full-grown tree quickly, don't lose track of what *weedy* means. It means that the tree will grow fast without holding to a pretty form. A straggly or thickety tree works well for an informal area of the garden, but in more refined places you'll need to prune it and keep pruning it, and it will most probably grow beyond your ladders, so you'll be hiring an arborist to keep it in shape. He or she will for sure advise you to get rid of the tree, because it's weedy. Weedy trees are often brittle, which means branches that frame views may come down in a storm or the trunk may split. Often they are short-lived, which gives you an opportunity to make a better choice the second time around.

*Aggressive* or *invasive roots* are words that may mean lawsuits. Roots that can find their way through concrete foundations and sidewalks and drainage pipes are liabilities that are often overlooked because they are out of sight. Beware of poplars. And, to be cautious, don't plant trees very close to walls.

## CONTAINER, BARE-ROOT, OR BALLED-AND-BURLAPPED?

€€€ Most trees available to the home gardener are growing in containers, 1-gallon, 5-gallon, or, more rarely, 15-gallon size. They were started in the ground or in small containers on tree farms and potted into the sales container generally a year before being shipped to a nursery for sale. Container-grown trees are the most expensive and the most convenient. You can plant one at any time of the year, provided your soil is workable (not frozen or flooded).

Bare-root trees are available only during late fall, winter, and very early spring. They look like leafless sticks, because they are dormant, and the roots have no soil around them (they do have moist sawdust or other material to keep them moist during transit). They were dug from the ground at a tree farm in the fall, and the soil was washed off before shipping. Bare-root trees are easier to plant than the other kinds, because they are lighter to handle. They are also less expensive to buy. Mail-order companies often ship bare-root trees. Fruit trees were always sold bare-root in the past.

Balled-and-burlapped (b&b) trees are also dormant and available only from late fall to early spring. They were dug up at a tree farm in fall with a ball of soil around their roots and wrapped in burlap for shipping. Very large trees in commercial landscape projects are often b&b trees. The soil ball is clay and therefore quite heavy.

## CHOOSING A HEALTHY CONTAINER-GROWN TREE €€€

Even if you've never bought a tree before, you'll know a healthy container-grown tree when you see one. It's what you had in your mind's eye—clean, good-sized leaves on strong branches, and the branches evenly balanced, not crossing one another or all growing in one direction, so that the shape is handsome from all sides.

If the tree has been through hard times already, it will show. Reject trees that have injuries to the bark or broken branches. Also reject trees if the leaves seem small or are wilting; the roots are probably too small to provide sufficient water or have been broken or shaken loose from the soil during transit.

The state of the roots is as telling as the look of the leaves and bark. Roots trailing through the drainage holes at the bottom of the container are a bad sign; the tree has been too long in the container. The same is true if roots are bulging from the surface of the soil or, even worse, coiling around the trunk. If the tree hasn't spent enough time in the container, it will feel loose, and the soil may be spilling from the container. Reject these trees, because the writing is on the wall that they won't grow well once they're planted, however much you pamper them.

CHOOSING A HEALTHY BARE-ROOT TREE ⋘ An excellent bare-root tree is fully dormant, with no buds beginning to open, or new white roots beginning to grow. It has well-developed roots radiating out on all sides from the trunk, not circling around one another, and healthy firm roots, not damaged or dry withered ones. Check also that the branches are healthy, not thin or shriveled or broken.

CHOOSING A HEALTHY BALLED-AND-BURLAPPED TREE ⋘ A healthy b&b tree is fully dormant, with no sign of leaves or flowers. The tree trunk should be firmly attached to the rootball, not wobbling, and the rootball should be one solid piece, without cracks or loose soil, which would indicate that the soil had dried out. Check that the branches are healthy, not thin or shriveled or broken.

CHOOSING A TREE FOR ITS FORM ⋘ A copse of maples planted informally may benefit from variety in the forms of the trees—some leaning, some low-branching, some a little lanky—because copses in the natural landscape are this way, and irregularity best evokes them. However, a formal grove of trees set out in geometric lines needs to look uniform, so choose trees of the same height, same age, same vigor; the one gawky one will always stand out. A lopsided tree may be useful if you are planting it near a wall. If you are buying a tree for a focal point, it may not do at all.

CHOOSING THE SIZE OF TREE ❮❮❮ We all really want an instant garden, want to see now what the trees will look like in five years, daydream of the dappled light that will flicker over the patio and the day when we'll look up into a ceiling of living foliage or take shelter there from a summer shower. But most people who love gardening, or have some faith that they will love gardening, do not special-order gigantic trees and pay a month's salary for them, because there's not much gardening fun in that.

Trees, even slow-growing ones, put on substantial growth each year. For a tree, 1 foot on each branch is moderate growth, so each year the change is noticeable: the shade spreads, the shadows reach the path before you've thought about it, and the foliage will be waving over your skylights before too long. It's an enormous pleasure to watch a tree grow, especially if you planted it as a small bare stick.

Trees that do best are the healthiest ones from the start, so buy freshly arrived, well-grown, and well-handled trees from the best nurseries, and don't worry a bit if they're 3 feet tall or 6. From all the stories you hear, the small overtake the tall, and they are much easier to transport and plant.

BRINGING TREES HOME ❮❮❮ Many healthy trees lose their health on the way home from the nursery. The trees you see in the backs of trucks, their branches and leaves thrashing about in the wind, are becoming desiccated very fast and may not ever be the same. If you're transporting a container tree in full leaf in an open truck, mist the foliage and wrap it in something windproof before leaving the nursery. Bare-root and b&b trees need careful handling too; the roots must never dry out, so be sure they are wrapped well before you drive off.

WHEN TO PLANT ❮❮❮ There's no particular season for planting container trees, although most gardeners do it in early spring or early fall, because these are the seasons when the soil is easy to dig and warm enough to help the roots get off to a good start. If you plant in summer, wait for a cool windless day, when there's less danger of the roots drying out while you're planting, and be religiously careful about watering the tree regularly in hot weather. In winter, wait for a dry period, because tramping over the soil when it's wet damages the soil.

Plant bare-root and b&b trees in fall, as soon as they are available, or in very early spring before they break dormancy. At these times, the roots have a chance to grow for a while, the better to supply water and nutrients to the leaves and flowers when they emerge.

PLANTING A CONTAINER-GROWN TREE ≪≪≪ Most trees grown for the home gardener are available in rigid plastic or metal containers. Planting one is pretty much the same as planting a rose or lavender for the flower garden, though you may need a friend's help if the tree is heavy. (The recipes in the following chapters include instructions for planting from containers.)

Before you start, water the tree in its container and see Digging the Planting Hole on page 36 and Amending the Planting Soil on page 37. Try to slip the tree out of its container by turning the container on its side and gently pulling it away from the tree. Yanking on the trunk always seems like a good idea, but resist doing this, because, as the trunk takes the strain, the roots will break away from the rootball. Give the container sides and base a few sharp raps if the tree doesn't slide out easily. If necessary, cut away the container with a sharp knife; slit the container from rim to base in several places, being careful not to cut through any big roots with the knife.

If you are buying the tree from a nursery and planting it as soon as you get home, ask the nursery, as a favor, to cut the sides of the container and retie them with string. Be sure to keep the rootball moist and covered with damp cloths or newspapers if you have to delay planting. It's important to the growth of the tree that the rootball never dry out.

Take a hard look at the rootball once it's out of the container (mist the roots so they don't dry out while you're deliberating). Some surgery is necessary if the tree has become rootbound from growing too long in a small container. Matted and circling roots must be pried or cut loose and spread out, so that they will grow into the surrounding soil. Spray soil away from the rootball if necessary, and don't worry about breaking small roots on the edge of the rootball or unraveling the rootball a little; this work is critical to the future growth of the tree. If some roots are set on circling the rootball like corkscrews and won't be redirected, cut them back, because they will strangle the tree when it's in the ground.

Set the tree into the planting hole, lifting it with one hand on the trunk, one under the rootball. Fill in around the rootball with the soil you dug from the hole, working it firmly between the roots. Check that the tree is perfectly upright and that the rootball extends at least 1 inch above the soil surface (some arborists plant so that the rootball extends 3 inches above the soil surface, even 5 inches above if the soil is heavy, to be sure the tree won't settle too deeply in the loosened soil). Mound soil around the exposed rootball to cover the roots. Tamp, or press, the mound and the backfill soil firmly around the tree. The tamping is important, because the roots need to be in contact with the moist soil, not surrounded by air pockets. Make a watering moat (described on page 37), and water the tree thoroughly.

Water the tree regularly for the first growing season. The soil 1 inch below the surface should never dry out. Even if the tree is a drought-tolerant species, it needs regular watering to get established.

PLANTING A BARE-ROOT TREE ⋘ A bare-root tree is easy to plant successfully as long as you take care of one item of business: keep the roots covered and moist from the moment you buy the plant until it is in the ground. If the peat, sawdust, or other material around the roots during transport starts to dry out, moisten it with spray from the hose, and, while you are digging the planting hole, keep the tree in a bucket of water. A dry environment, especially on a hot or windy day, will desiccate the roots and kill the tree. (If a tree arrives with dry, shriveled roots, call the supplier, and send it back.)

If you can't plant immediately, "heel in" the tree—dig a shallow hole in the ground, lay down the tree so that its roots are in the hole, cover the roots with soil, and keep the soil moist until you can plant.

The night before planting, place the tree roots in a bucket of water (keep it in the garage if the water could freeze outdoors); this hydration process seems to help the tree get away to a good start.

Dig the planting hole (see page 36). At the center of the hole, build a mound of firm soil on which to place the tree.

Before planting, prune away any broken or damaged roots. If the tree needs staking—because you're planting in a windy site or the young trunk isn't holding itself upright very well—hammer a single stake into the soil 9 to 12 inches from the center of the mound. Place it on the windward side of the tree: stand facing the planting hole with your back to the prevailing wind, and place the stake between yourself and the planting mound. Staking isn't advised unless it's necessary (see page 38).

Place the tree in the hole, on the mound, and spread the roots out radially. Fill in around the roots with the soil you dug from the hole, wiggling it in among the roots carefully and firmly with a chopstick or a bamboo stake. Check that the tree is perfectly upright, and that the old soil line on the trunk sits at least 1 inch above the soil surface. Tamp, or press, the soil firmly around the tree. The tamping is important, because the roots need to be in contact with the moist soil, not surrounded by air pockets. Make a watering moat (see page 37), and water the tree thoroughly.

Check the stake. It should be very firm in the ground, and its top should sit just below the lowest branches. Trim the stake if necessary. Secure the tree to the stake with a proper tree tie—a belt and buckle tie or a flexible plastic tree tie looped in a figure eight—that prevents the tree trunk from hitting against the stake. A flexible tie is perhaps best, because it's so easy to forget to loosen other ties, and they damage the trunk if they become too tight.

After planting, a bare-root tree does not need much watering until the leaves appear. Figure on keeping the soil damp, not wet, because if the root zone becomes soggy, new roots will be slow to form. Come spring and warm weather, you need to water more often and continue watering regularly for the first growing season. The soil 1 inch below the surface should never dry out. Even if the tree is a drought-tolerant species, it needs regular watering to get established.

PLANTING A BALLED AND BURLAPPED TREE ⋘ A b&b tree is usually too heavy for one person to manage easily, so solicit help from a friend to avoid hurting your back. Unlike the soil in a standard container, which is light so that it's easier and less expensive to transport, the soil under the burlap is usually heavy clay, the better to hold together in one piece during transport.

Handle the tree carefully. If the soil ball crumbles, the roots may become exposed to air pockets and dry out. Keep the burlap moist from the moment you buy the tree until it is planted.

When you are ready to plant (see Digging the Planting Hole on page 36 and Amending the Planting Soil on page 37), place the tree alongside the hole, and remove the burlap, the strings, and the ties. With a friend's help, one pair of hands under the rootball, another steadying the trunk, lower the tree into the hole. Try not to maneuver the tree by its trunk, because, as the trunk rocks, the roots will break away from the rootball. If it's easier to place the tree in the hole with its burlap and then remove the burlap, cutting it away as best you can, do that. It doesn't matter if some burlap is left under the rootball.

Half fill the hole with the soil you dug from the hole, and tamp the soil gently with your foot. Check that the tree is upright, fill the hole, and tamp once more. The tamping is important, because the roots need to be in contact with the moist soil, not surrounded by air pockets. Make a watering moat (see page 37), and water the tree thoroughly.

Water the tree regularly for the first growing season. The soil 1 inch below the surface should never dry out. Even if the tree is a drought-tolerant species, it needs regular watering to get established.

DIGGING THE PLANTING HOLE ⋘ Dig the planting hole wide—two or three times wider than the extent of the roots—but don't dig it deep. The tree will grow better if it sits high on a firm support of undug soil. If the soil directly under the tree is loose, the tree will sink as the soil settles, and a tree planted too deeply is prone to problems.

Place a bamboo stake against the tree to gauge how deep the hole must be to accommodate the root system, and mark the stake. For a container-grown tree and a balled-and-burlapped tree, measure from the top to the bottom of the rootball, first brushing aside any debris or loose soil that may have collected around the trunk. For a bare-root tree, measure from the old soil mark, usually obvious by a change in color at the base of the trunk, to the root tips.

The rule of thumb is to make the hole 1 inch shallower than the root system, so that the trunk-to-root juncture will sit 1 inch above the surrounding soil. If your soil is heavy and doesn't drain well, make the hole 3 inches shallower; when you've finished planting the tree you can mound soil over any protruding roots.

Once you have the hole dug properly to support the tree at the correct height, excavate with the spade or a trowel around the edges at the bottom of the hole so that the tree roots can grow down into loose soil, but be sure to leave a firm plateau for the tree to sit on. Then, as a last step, loosen the soil around the sides of the hole to help the tree roots penetrate easily into the surrounding soil.

AMENDING THE PLANTING SOIL ⋘ The new rule of thumb is not to amend the backfill, or planting, soil, because it can discourage the tree's roots from growing beyond the planting hole. For best growth, the soil around the young roots and in the surrounding area should be fairly uniform.

If you are planting a bare-root tree, the guidelines are simple: backfill with the soil you dug from the hole, without adding anything to it. If you are planting a container-grown tree or a balled-and-burlapped tree, the recommendation is also for no amendments, unless your garden soil is significantly different from the soil already around the tree roots.

Most container trees are growing in a light and porous soil that drains well. If your garden soil is clay, which absorbs water slowly, irrigation water may collect in the porous soil of the tree's rootball after planting and drown the tree. Reduce this risk by adding organic matter such as ground bark to the backfill soil, one shovelful to every two shovelfuls of original soil.

The roots of balled-and-burlapped trees are in heavy clay soil. If you have a light sandy soil, you can hose most of the heavy soil away from the roots, provided the tree is not sensitive to root disturbance, or you can add organic matter to the backfill soil, as described above, to create a transition zone.

MAKING A WATERING MOAT ⋘ Make a watering moat by building a 4-inch-high dike of soil around the planting hole. Water the newly planted tree slowly and thoroughly. Then recheck the position of the tree; if it has settled too close to the surrounding soil line or below it, remove some soil, gently lift the tree and jiggle the soil through its roots until the tree is at the correct depth. If you've planted very high because your soil is heavy, cover any protruding roots with a mound of soil.

PRUNING AFTER PLANTING ⋘ It used to be common to prune the top of the tree immediately after planting to compensate for the stress the root system suffers during planting, but experts now advise that you leave the top of the tree just as it is. However, if any twigs are broken, do prune those.

MULCHING ⋘ Mulching helps reduce evaporation from the soil surface and discourages weeds; organic mulches also provide some nutrition.
Spread a 3-inch layer of woody organic material, such as shredded bark (not
fresh organic material such as new grass clippings or manure) in the watering
moat, keeping it 6 inches away from the base of the trunk. Apply new mulch
every spring, over the top of the old mulch and out over a wider area to keep
pace with the growing roots, always leaving the space around the trunk bare,
so as not to attract nibbling rodents.

STAKING TREES ⋘ Most trees are best left *unstaked*, to grow stout
and strongly anchored on their own. The only trees that need to be protected
from falling over in the wind are willowy, slender-trunked trees with heavy
tops of foliage and trees with reputations for becoming uprooted. (In the
recipes in the following chapters, trees that need staking are identified.)

Landscape contractors use different staking methods. Sometimes you'll
see a single stake close to the tree trunk, which is a simple method suitable for
small bare-root trees (see Planting a Bare-Root Tree on page 34).

Two stakes are better, because they brace the tree away from both stakes
and you can place them beyond the rootball to avoid damaging any of the
roots. Use round tree stakes or pieces of two-by-two. You'll probably need
6- to 7-foot lengths—the length of the tree trunk from the soil surface to just
below the lowest branches, plus 1 to 2 feet below ground.

In windy situations, first figure out the direction of the prevailing wind.
Stand with your back to it, and place the first stake in front of you, 1 foot from
the trunk, and the second on the other side of the trunk, directly across from
the first. Hammer them 1 to 2 feet into the ground, until they are very firm.

It's tempting to tie the ties good and tight, but don't. Some give will allow
the tree a chance to rock a little in the wind and strengthen its trunk and root
system so that the tree is better prepared for a gale. Tight ties, if forgotten for
a season, will also bite into the bark.

Expandable plastic tree ties are best. Ordinary plastic or wire-and-rubber
ties must be adjusted regularly. People often forget about the ties and the
stakes. Stakes should be removed after the first year or, at most, two years.

TREE WRAPS ‹‹‹ It's questionable whether tree wraps prevent sunburn, or sunscald, of the trunk. You might, however, paint the trunk with white latex (water-based) paint, as much for its Mediterranean effect as its practical benefit.

It does make sense to protect the young tree from foraging deer and rabbits and from pets if you foresee a problem. Chicken wire works well. Hammer three stakes into the ground, at least 1 foot from the trunk, and attach a cylinder of chicken wire to the stakes.

WATERING TREES ‹‹‹ A tree takes a couple of years to establish itself after planting. During this time, water it regularly through the dry season, perhaps weekly in its first year, and at other times as necessary to keep the soil damp 1 or 2 inches below the surface. Water even drought-tolerant trees this way until they are established.

Once the tree has a good set of anchoring and feeding roots spread far through the soil, less frequent water is needed. Just how much and how often depends on the tree and your climate. A drought-tolerant tree and any tree native to your area will obviously grow with little or no irrigation once it's established but will probably be lusher and prettier if you water it two or three times during the dry season.

During the first year, water the tree by placing a hose in the watering moat. In subsequent years, water a larger and larger area as the tree roots spread. Let a hose flow at the lowest trickle for an hour at the base of the tree; then move the hose to one or two other spots for an additional hour. Or set up a drip irrigation system with a loop of emitters around the tree, choosing emitters that will deliver the water slowly so that it soaks deeply into the root zone. Avoid frequent shallow watering; you don't want to encourage the roots to grow close to the surface.

Some mature trees, especially oaks, are sensitive to changes in watering; irrigating new ground cover or a new lawn laid anywhere near such a tree could kill it.

Don't overwater drought-tolerant trees; some are sensitive to too much water, and won't survive, for example, in a lawn that you water two or three times a week through summer. Other trees require regular watering and flourish in lawns or flower and shrub borders that are watered regularly. In cold-winter climates, water trees, especially evergreens, well in late fall if the soil is dry. The recipes that follow indicate how much water the trees need.

### FERTILIZING TREES ⋘
Ornamental trees generally do not need fertilizer. In spring, you will know that your trees are doing fine if they put out sturdy new growth with good-sized healthy leaves. If that's the case, you can simply let them be, seeking their nutrients deep and far through the native soil and appreciating the nutrients in the mulch you lay every year (see page 38).

If you want to pamper a tree, keep up with the mulching schedule. Many arborists do not recommend granular nitrogen fertilizers. They are like steroids in boosting growth unnaturally and can cause damage in the long run by thinning the tree's cell walls. If a tree starts to show signs of trouble, and no pests or diseases are evident, the soil may be lacking in some important nutrient. Call an arborist or your county cooperative extension office for advice; these experts can test your soil or refer you to a soil-testing lab.

### PRUNING UP YOUNG TREES AND SHRUB-TREES ⋘
Wait at least a year after planting a tree before you start to prune it up (remove branches that are too low on the trunk), and then prune the lowest branches in stages; if you cut them right back to the trunk immediately, the trunk may become weak and spindly. In late winter or early spring, cut back the lowest branches by about one-third to side branches, leaving no stubs. The following winter or early spring, remove those lowest branches entirely and cut back the higher branches by one-third, and so on, year by year, until the trunk is clear to the desired height. Ornamental trees usually have 4 to 6 feet of clear trunk. Shade trees need 8 feet of clear trunk, for people to walk under them.

After pruning up, your tree may need pruning in the future only to remove dead or broken branches. To allow the tree to take its natural form (usually the most beautiful), prune only when necessary. If you want to train your tree to frame a porch or a distant view, consider meeting with an experienced arborist while the tree is still young.

### BUZZ-CUT PRUNING AND TOPPING ⋘
Don't buzz-cut or top a tree, because its natural form will be ruined permanently. And this cutting won't reduce the height of the tree; in fact, the tree will grow with even

greater vigor, producing a thicket of strong upright shoots at every cut. Buzz-cutting is for formal hedges; the way to prune a tree is to thin it.

A tree that's too tall visually can be integrated into the garden by under-planting it with smaller trees, and underplanting those with shrubs (see the recipe on page 94). Or you can treat the bare trunk as structure and decorate it with vines. If a tree is casting too much shade, thin it.

THINNING TREES ⋘ Thinning a tree means removing branches, cutting them back either to side branches or to the trunk. A tree growing too large for its space can often be contained by removing some of the heavier branches in this way; the process is called drop crotching. If you leave no stubs and no sharp elbows (don't cut back to a sharp-angled side branch or one significantly thinner than the one you're removing), and you choose your cuts wisely, your tree will continue to look natural in form. However, most of us don't have a clear sense of how a particular tree will grow if we cut it here or there, and once you begin to saw, the changes are irrevocable. Take a tree pruning class or ask a tree supplier to recommend a professional tree pruner. Don't wait for the tree to outgrow its space; the pruning needs to start when the tree is approaching the size you'd like it to stay.

Thin a tree in summer if you are trying to contain its growth. The new growth won't be as vigorous as it would be after early spring pruning. Sum-mer is also the time to remove suckers sprouting from the base of the tree and water sprouts, those strong upright shoots that grow rapidly on the branches and trunks of some trees.

PRUNING CUTS ⋘ The best tool for pruning branches is a pruning saw, not a lopper. Hand pruners are good only for branches about ½ inch thick. If the branch is heavy, don't try to juggle holding it and making the cut. Saw off the branch leaving a 4- or 6-inch stub, first undercutting it, so that it doesn't tear. Then remove the stub with a fine careful cut, keeping ½ inch away from the branch collar, the slight swelling underneath the branch where it meets the trunk, and leaving a ¼-inch lip on the top side of the branch. If you've left any stub that you could hang something on, you haven't pruned close enough to the trunk. The wound will heal best without any paints or wound treatments.

# CENTERPIECES, ONE OF A KIND

A single cherry tree with flowers opening along bare branches on an otherwise wintry day will draw you down the garden path over wet stones and splattering raindrops. The white-pink petals emerge from red bud cases and smell faintly of spring and rain. The light swells under the tree, refracted off the flowers.

The same tree closes down the gardening season in fall. A skirt of yellow-orange leaves settles on the garden floor around its trunk. In the mornings, it's covered with dew or frost. The branches lift with the wind, gray stippled wood against gunmetal-gray sky, the last colorful leaves holding on, and buds already plumping for next spring's flowers.

Choose a tree that is handsome all year for a garden centerpiece, and place it at a focal point—at the destination of a path or a corner in a path—to pull people to that point (and then perhaps on to the next); or at the house entrance or back door; or to soften the lines of an outbuilding; or, for the pleasure of watching it through rainstorms and sunsets, in line with the kitchen or the living room window.

Many common trees make fine centerpieces. Instead of an expensive wedding cake novelty with pink-variegated leaves, glassy bark, and double flowers, consider a tree closer to nature. The garden in the photograph here was built around the old apple tree. Carefully pruned and shaggy with moss, it catches the eye even when it's not flowering or fruiting.

# GOLD KATSURA,
# PURPLE ADIRONDACKS

*After a cold night in early fall, this katsura tree begins its long, two-tone journey from green to gold. The green retreats differently from each pretty, penny-round leaf, fading plain away on some, on others leaving bright zigzagging bars and Rorschach blots among the glowing yellow.*

*There comes a time when the branches are veiled with pure gold, all the leaves present and perfect, strung in pairs on twigs as fine as wire. Days pass, fog burning off into sunshine, then rain. The leaves flutter from their long leafstalks, smelling of cotton candy. Then they start to drift into the emerald grass and fill the seats of the Adirondack chairs no longer warmed by the sun.*

*Slants of wintry light reach the floors inside the house as the leaves fall, and delicate, open branch patterns flicker over bedspreads and fireplaces.*

# HOW TO DO IT ◄◄◄

This katsura (*Cercidiphyllum japonicum*) is 15 years old. It may grow to 50 feet tall; in a small garden, be prepared to prune it, perhaps annually, to contain its size (see page 41).

Mark the planting site. Place the tree at least 5 feet from a building (8 or 10 feet would be better). Water the tree in its container. (If your tree is not in a container, see the instructions for planting bare-root and b&b trees, on pages 34 and 35.)

Dig the planting hole. Make it three times as wide but not quite as deep as the container. The tree will grow better if the top of its rootball sits 1 inch above the surrounding soil (3 inches above if your soil doesn't drain well). Leaving a plateau of firm soil for the tree to sit on, dig 2 inches deeper around the edges of the hole so that the roots can grow down into loose soil. Loosen the soil around the sides of the hole to help the roots penetrate laterally.

Remove the tree from its container. Try to slip it out by turning the container on its side and gently pulling it away from the plant. Don't yank on the trunk. Give the sides and base of the container a few sharp raps if the tree doesn't slide out easily. Cut away the container if necessary; slit it from rim to base in several places, being careful that you don't cut through any big roots.

Take a hard look at the rootball. If the roots are matted or circling the rootball, pry or cut them loose. Don't worry about breaking small roots on the edge of the rootball.

Set the tree into the planting hole, lifting it with one hand on the trunk, one under the rootball. Check that the top of the rootball is at least 1 inch above the soil surface. Fill in around the rootball with the soil you dug from the hole, working it firmly between the roots and lifting the tree if necessary to keep it above soil level. Mound soil around the exposed rootball to cover the roots. Press the soil firmly around the tree.

Make a watering moat by building a 4-inch-high dike of soil around the planting hole. Water the tree thoroughly.

Inexpensive
Easy
Location: Full sun or partial shade
Soil: Well-drained, rich; best fall color in acid soils
Tree hardiness: Zones 4–8

**Tools**
Measuring tape
Hose or watering can
Straight-edged spade
Trowel
Sharp knife

**Ingredients**
1 katsura tree (*Cercidiphyllum japonicum*)

**Maintenance**
Water tree regularly; it cannot withstand drought

# DOGWOOD ENTRANCE GARDEN

The dogwood tree is nicely mussing up a lot of architectural lines. It's a woodland tree, and when the wind blows, its branches softly lift and roll on the updrafts, obscuring the angles where the walls and roofs meet. In late spring, the otherwise formal entrance is mobbed by hundreds of soft white saucers draping around tiny button cups of green flowers.

The lawn and boxwood hedges stay a neat, calm, permanent green, while the tree follows its woodland nature. In September, the first patches of orange and red creep over the leaf surfaces, and the leaves rustle more dryly in the fresh wind. Then they start to skitter over the porch, a melee of dewy red and pink curls. In winter, the lines of the path, walls, and roof are overlaid with shadows of bare gray branches.

## HOW TO DO IT ⋘

This Eddie's White Wonder dogwood (*Cornus florida* x *C. nuttallii* 'Eddie's White Wonder') is 10 years old. It may grow to 20 or 30 feet. To keep the canopy from growing high above a low roof, be prepared to prune the tree, perhaps annually (see page 41). Several species of dogwood are available. This hybrid has very large bracts and reliable fall color in mild climates but may not always flower prolifically in zones 5 and 6. In those zones, if you have an acid soil, consider Kousa dogwood *(C. kousa).*

Choose a sheltered position for the tree; dogwoods do not thrive in windy conditions. Place the tree at least 4 feet from any walls.

Water the tree in its container. (If your tree is not in a container, see the instructions for planting bare-root and b&b trees, on pages 34 and 35.)

Dig the planting hole. Make it three times as wide but not quite as deep as the container. The tree will grow better if the top of its rootball sits 1 inch above the surrounding soil. Leaving a plateau of firm soil for the tree to sit on, dig 2 inches deeper around the edges of the hole so that the roots can grow down into loose soil. Loosen the soil around the sides of the hole to help the roots penetrate laterally.

Remove the tree from its container. Try to slip it out by turning the container on its side and gently pulling it away from the plant. Don't yank on the trunk. Give the sides and base of the container a few sharp raps if the tree doesn't slide out easily. Cut away the container if necessary; slit it from rim to base in several places, being careful that you don't cut through any big roots.

Try to disturb the rootball as little as possible, and once the tree is out of the container, plant it quickly or keep it covered with moist newspapers or cloth so that the roots do not dry out.

Set the tree into the planting hole, lifting it with one hand on the trunk, one under the rootball. Check that the top of the rootball is at least 1 inch above the soil surface. Fill in around the rootball with the soil you dug from the hole, working it firmly between the roots and lifting the tree if necessary to keep it above soil level. Mound soil around the exposed rootball to cover the roots. Press the soil firmly around the tree.

Make a watering moat by building a 4-inch-high dike of soil around the planting hole. Water the tree thoroughly.

Make a boxwood hedge (optional): Plant the boxwood plants in the same manner, but don't worry about making a plateau in the planting hole, and set the rootballs just ½ inch above soil level. Space the plants 9 inches apart.

Inexpensive
Easy
Location: Full sun or light shade
Soil: Well-drained, preferably a little acid
Tree hardiness: Zones 5–9

**Tools**
Measuring tape
Hose or watering can
Straight-edged spade
Trowel
Sharp knife
Moist newspapers or cloths, if necessary
    (see text)

**Ingredients**
1 Eddie's White Wonder dogwood
    (*Cornus florida* x *C. nuttallii* 'Eddie's
    White Wonder')
Boxwood hedge (optional), 4 plants
    (*Buxus* spp.) per 1 yard of border

**Maintenance**
Water tree regularly; it cannot withstand
    drought
In hot-summer climates, place bark mulch
    around tree to retain soil moisture
Call a professional pruner as tree ap-
    proaches desired height
Clip boxwood (optional) once or twice
    a year

# OLD SHED WITH REDBUD

An old shed has been transformed with a simple deck and arbor and a native redbud tree that is beautiful in every season. In spring, its bright wine-red pea flowers bloom right out of the brown bark along the delicate branches. From almost every reach of the garden, a branch of red blossom is visible against the sky.

Soon a scrim of glossy round leaves appears, fluttering in the lightest breeze. The deck becomes a hideaway for the duration of summer; sounds from the rest of the garden arrive as from far away, shadows play across the floor, and the light filtering in through chlorophyll is green.

In fall, layers of yellow and yellow-green leaves collect on the deck, and the dainty branches are revealed once more. Seedpods have formed now—brown beans that will click against each other during winter storms.

# HOW TO DO IT ⋘

This redbud is *Cercis* 'Oklahoma,' sometimes sold as *C. canadensis* 'Oklahoma' or *C. reniformis* 'Oklahoma.' It is 10 years old and may grow to 20 feet tall and equally wide. Redbud species are available with white, pink, or rosy purple flowers. *C. canadensis* 'Forest Pansy,' a purple-leafed species, needs some shade in hot climates. Under the tree are maiden's wreath plants, which produce spikes of white flowers in midsummer, and yellow daylilies, which bloom all summer.

Mark the planting site. Place the tree at least 4 feet from a building. Water the tree in its container. (If your tree is not in a container, see the instructions for planting bare-root and b&b trees, on pages 34 and 35.)

Dig the planting hole. Make it three times as wide but not quite as deep as the container. The tree will grow better if the top of its rootball sits 1 inch above the surrounding soil (3 inches above if your soil doesn't drain well). Leaving a plateau of firm soil for the tree to sit on, dig 2 inches deeper around the edges of the hole so that the roots can grow down into loose soil. Loosen the soil around the sides of the hole to help the roots penetrate laterally.

Remove the tree from its container. Try to slip it out by turning the container on its side and gently pulling it away from the plant. Don't yank on the trunk. Give the sides and base of the container a few sharp raps if the tree doesn't slide out easily. Cut away the container if necessary; slit it from rim to base in several places, being careful that you don't cut through any big roots.

Take a hard look at the rootball. If the roots are matted or circling the rootball, pry or cut them loose. Don't worry about breaking small roots on the edge of the rootball.

Set the tree into the planting hole, lifting it with one hand on the trunk, one under the rootball. Check that the top of the rootball is at least 1 inch above the soil surface. Fill in around the rootball with the soil you dug from the hole, working it firmly between the roots and lifting the tree if necessary to keep it above soil level. Mound soil around the exposed rootball to cover the roots. Press the soil firmly around the tree.

Make a watering moat by building a 4-inch-high dike of soil around the planting hole. Water the tree thoroughly.

Plant the maiden's wreath and daylilies in the same manner, but don't worry about making a plateau in the planting hole, and set the rootballs just ½ inch above soil level. Space the plants 18 inches apart, the maiden's wreath in the front of the garden, the daylilies at the back.

Inexpensive
Easy
Location: Full sun or light shade
Soil: Most soils, except wet heavy ones
Tree hardiness: Zones 5–9, maybe zone 4

**Tools**
Measuring tape
Hose or watering can
Straight-edged spade
Trowel
Sharp knife

**Ingredients**
1 redbud (*Cercis* spp.)
Maiden's wreath (*Francoa ramosa*) for foreground, 4 per square yard
Daylilies (*Hemerocallis* 'Stella D'Oro' or other variety) for background, 4 per square yard

**Maintenance**
Water tree and perennials regularly until established, then moderately
Fertilize perennials in spring and mid-summer
Divide perennials every third year, in early spring

# WHITE CRAPE WALKWAY

In the first days of spring, the cracks of the flagstone floor under the columned walkway fill with fragrant sweet violets. Swags of wisteria vine follow, descending from the beams and releasing scented petals into the air. By May, the columns frame the intricately pleated ruby-red and lacy pink teacups of headily perfumed old roses.

While the rose petals are still drifting among the stones in the path, onto the summer stage bursts the grand finale—a treetop of crinkly white crape myrtle blossoms. The tips of the branches dip with the weight of the giant fragrant cones, up to 12 inches long. The blossoms fade only when the leaves turn yellow-orange in fall and start to fall among the mottled pink-cinnamon tree trunks.

HOW TO DO IT ⋘ This crape myrtle (*Lagerstroemia* 'Natchez,' a mildew- and aphid-resistant hybrid from the U.S. National Arboretum) is a multi-trunked tree 10 years old. It may grow to 20 feet tall but can be kept smaller by winter pruning. One tree makes a focal point or centerpiece of the arbor, but pairs of trees could be planted across the walkway from each other, between the columns. Maiden grasses flank the tree. Varieties of crape myrtle are available with pink, lavender, purple, or deep-red flowers.

The arbor is a moderately expensive construction of eight stucco columns, each 8 feet tall, and substantial overhead beams. It covers a generous pathway, 10 feet wide and 20 feet long, paved with flagstones and an edging of tile. Consider hiring a landscape architect or contractor to build the arbor and lay the floor. The arbor must be strong enough to bear the very considerable weight of a mature wisteria vine. Leave 4-inch spaces between the flagstones, for the violets.

Mark the location for the tree. Place it midway between two columns of the walkway, at least 2 feet from the walkway edge.

Water the tree in its container. (If your tree is not in a container, see the instructions for planting bare-root and b&b trees, on pages 34 and 35.)

Dig the planting hole. Make it three times as wide but not quite as deep as the container. The tree will grow better if the top of its rootball sits 1 inch above the surrounding soil (3 inches above if your soil doesn't drain well). Leaving a plateau of firm soil for the tree to sit on, dig 2 inches deeper around the edges of the hole so that the roots can grow down into loose soil. Loosen the soil around the sides of the hole to help the roots penetrate laterally.

Remove the tree from its container. Try to slip it out by turning the container on its side and gently pulling it away from the plant. Don't yank on the trunk. Give the sides and base of the container a few sharp raps if the tree doesn't slide out easily. Cut away the container if necessary; slit it from rim to base in several places, being careful that you don't cut through any big roots.

Take a hard look at the rootball. If the

Moderately expensive
Moderately easy
Location: Full sun, hot summers
Soil: Most kinds, except very dry or
  very wet ones
Tree hardiness: Zones 7–9

**Tools**

Measuring tape
Hose or watering can
Straight-edged spade
Trowel
Sharp knife
Plastic ties for wisteria shoots
Pruning shears

**Ingredients**

Arbor and flagstone walkway (see text)
1 multi-trunked Natchez crape myrtle
  (*Lagerstroemia* 'Natchez')
Sweet violets (*Viola odorata*), in six-packs,
  2 plants per foot of paving crack
Shrub roses, 1 per square yard
2 miscanthus grasses (*Miscanthus sinensis*)
1 wisteria vine (*Wisteria* spp.)

**Maintenance**

Water all plants regularly until established, then moderately
Remove any suckers that grow from base of tree
Cut back grasses close to ground before growth starts in spring
Fertilize violets in spring, before flowering begins
Fertilize wisteria in spring and summer until it's well grown, then stop fertilizing
Prune roses annually, before growth starts in spring
Fertilize roses through growing season
Train wisteria shoots over walkway; tie them to beams

roots are matted or circling the rootball, pry or cut them loose. Don't worry about breaking small roots on the edge of the rootball.

Set the tree into the planting hole, lifting it with one hand on the trunk, one under the rootball. Check that the top of the rootball is at least 1 inch above the soil surface. Fill in around the rootball with the soil you dug from the hole, working it firmly between the roots and lifting the tree if necessary to keep it above soil level. Mound soil around the exposed rootball to cover the roots. Press the soil firmly around the tree.

Make a watering moat by building a 4-inch-high dike of soil around the planting hole. Water the tree thoroughly.

Plant the violets, roses, grasses, and wisteria in the same manner, but don't worry about making a plateau in the planting hole, and set the rootballs just ½ inch above soil level. Space the violets 6 inches apart among the flagstones. Plant the roses 3 feet apart in a neighboring flower bed. Space the grasses 3 feet from the tree. Plant the wisteria at the foot of a column; wrap plastic ties around the pillar to hold the wisteria shoots in place until they reach the beams.

To prevent the tree from becoming shrubby, remove suckers that sprout from the base of the trunk, cutting them right back to the ground. To show off the bark, as the tree grows taller, shorten the lowest branches one winter and then the following winter cut them back to the trunk. To keep the tree small, trim the ends of the branches or remove entire branches. Prune in winter or early spring, before new growth starts; flowers bloom on the ends of new shoots, so don't wait until those shoots grow or you'll have fewer blooms.

# STRAWBERRY GUAVA, GRAVEL RIVER

In the passageway between the side of the house and the garden wall flows a river of gray gravel, with stepping stones that follow and cross it. Coming along the path, you pass a range of miniature mountains, with succulents growing in the crevices, cross an escarpment of rock over a narrow channel where the river must run deep, and then arrive at the calm shadowy lagoon where the river opens out under a strawberry guava tree.

The tree stands near the shore, with its smooth tan-and-gray–splashed trunk in the swirl, and its shiny, evergreen leaves waving over the garden wall. Leaves drop from the tree, as do fleshy edible fruits that ripen from dark red to almost black. A glass ball, a whirlpool of movement and color, spins with them on the river.

# HOW TO DO IT ⋘ This strawberry guava shrub-tree *(Psidium cattleianum)* is 17 years old. It has been pruned into this delicate dancing tree shape. The river is composed of fine gray gravel, while the banks are larger tan gravel. The moderately expensive elements in the composition are the mountain boulders and stepping-stone slabs; choose craggy mossy boulders that look like mountains in miniature and irregular river-washed stones in the shapes of islands and promontories. The boulders are too heavy for two people to move. Consider hiring someone who has the equipment to move them; the rock supplier will be able to give you leads.

Mark out the river course, using the twine and stakes. Bring it around the corner of the house flowing in a curve about 2½ to 3 feet wide, wider in the place where it turns, where the water would erode the outside bank. Along the passageway make it swing just once—toward the mountain range, around it, and back to within 2 feet of the wall. Have the river end in a soft-edged lagoon, about 5 feet wide. Lay the gravel later, once you've placed the boulders and stones and planted the tree.

Place the mountain boulders near the garden fence or wall, craggy sides facing the stepping-stone path. A sense of mass is best achieved by grouping the boulders so that they touch, in a line, like a mountain range. Bury the bottom third of the boulders; that way they'll seem to be part of the bedrock.

Place the stepping-stones. Experiment with a flowing line that follows the watercourse part of the way, then crosses it before the lagoon. Path and river will integrate beautifully if you jut stepping-stones well into the inside curves of the river, to give the impression that the water had to change course there, around solid rock. At the river crossing, make the river narrow, say 18 inches across, and place stepping-stones on opposite sides of the bank, to create a gorge.

Plant the tree where the river opens into the lagoon, in the water, about 9 inches from the river's edge. Water the tree in its container. (If your tree is not in a container, see the instructions for planting bare-root and b&b trees, on pages 34 and 35.)

Dig the planting hole. Make it three times as wide but not quite as deep as the container. The tree will grow better if the top of its rootball sits 1 inch above the surrounding soil. Leaving a plateau of firm soil for the tree to sit on, dig a few inches deeper around the edges of the hole so that the roots can

---

Moderately expensive
Moderately difficult
Location: Full sun or very light shade
Soil: Rich
Tree hardiness: Zones 8–9

**Tools**
2 balls of twine and bundle of bamboo
    or wooden stakes
Measuring tape
Hose or watering can
Straight-edged spade
Trowel
Sharp knife
Rake
Shovel

**Ingredients**
1 strawberry guava *(Psidium cattleianum)*
2 mountain-shaped boulders, with crags
    and crevices, each 4 feet across
Stepping-stones—river-washed irregular
    slabs—4 per 3-yard length of path
Gray gravel, ⅝- or ¾-inch, approx. 1½
    cubic feet per 1-yard length of water-
    course
Tan gravel, 2-inch, approx. 2¼ cubic feet
    per 1 square yard of bank
Potting soil, for planting boulder crevices
Succulent cuttings, for boulder crevices
2 Japanese anemones *(Anemone hybrida)*

**Maintenance**
Water tree and succulents regularly until
    established, then only occasionally
Water anemones regularly until estab-
    lished, then moderately
After second year, start to prune tree
    gradually to desired shape (see
    page 41)

grow down into loose soil. Loosen the soil around the sides of the hole to help the roots penetrate laterally.

Remove the tree from its container. Try to slip it out by turning the container on its side and gently pulling it away from the plant. Don't yank on the trunk. Give the sides and base of the container a few sharp raps if the tree doesn't slide out easily. Cut away the container if necessary; slit it from rim to base in several places, being careful that you don't cut through any big roots.

Take a hard look at the rootball. If the roots are matted or circling the rootball, pry or cut them loose. Don't worry about breaking small roots on the edge of the rootball.

Set the tree into the planting hole, lifting it with one hand on the trunk, one under the rootball. Check that the top of the rootball is 1 inch above the soil surface. Fill in around the rootball with the soil you dug from the hole, working it firmly between the roots and lifting the tree if necessary to keep it above soil level. Mound soil around the exposed rootball to cover the roots. Press the soil firmly around the tree. Water the tree thoroughly.

Review the lines of the watercourse. Check that the negative spaces, which you'll be covering with tan gravel, are nicely fluid in shape too.

Rake the soil the length of the passageway, and firm any areas you've disturbed while digging. Shovel the gray gravel onto the watercourse, and spread it evenly, 2 inches deep. Scatter a thin layer of gravel over the tree rootball, just enough to hide the soil, being careful not to scrape the bark of the tree.

Review the lines of the river once more, and make any changes now. Then spread the tan gravel 3 inches deep over the river banks, keeping the line crisp between bank and river, and the river lower than its banks.

Check the stepping-stones. If one wobbles or sits below the river surface, place it on a bed of gravel.

Pack the potting soil into any crevices in the mountains, and plant the cuttings of succulents there. Keep the crevices watered until the succulents are established; then water only rarely. To fill an odd-shaped corner between mountain range and wall, plant two Japanese anemones; the foliage will read as a forest.

Rake the river in the manner of a Japanese dry garden, leaving lines that swing through the curves.

# HARLEQUIN GLORYBOWER
# AND BIRDBATH

It's easy to rest here all afternoon in the sunshine, toes in the grass. There's nothing showy in this part of the garden demanding attention, just an occasional gust of the first yellow fall leaves spiraling down among gentle shades of green.

But sooner or later, maybe not until the sun goes down, the feet will follow cues the eyes have taken in—birds have been splashing in the birdbath at the end of the lawn all afternoon and fussing in the harlequin glorybower tree alongside. A mowed strip swings in that direction, so you take it, almost unthinking. The circle of sparkling water in the birdbath pulls you on. Then, suddenly, you've come upon a hoard of extraordinary fruits— branches sagging with metallic turquoise buttons studded into waxy red stars. A month earlier, fragrant white flowers hung from these red calyxes.

## HOW TO DO IT ‹‹‹ This harlequin glorybower (*Clerodendrum trichotomum*) is a single-trunked tree, 10 years old. It may grow to 15 feet. If you can find only a shrub form, consider pruning it up into a tree (see page 40). The birdbath sits alongside the tree, in the sun.

Water the tree in its container. (If your tree is not in a container, see the instructions for planting bare-root and b&b trees, on pages 34 and 35.)

Dig the planting hole. Make it three times as wide but not quite as deep as the container. The tree will grow better if the top of its rootball sits 1 inch above the surrounding soil (3 inches above if your soil doesn't drain well). Leaving a plateau of firm soil for the tree to sit on, dig 2 inches deeper around the edges of the hole so that the roots can grow down into loose soil. Loosen the soil around the sides of the hole to help the roots penetrate laterally.

Remove the tree from its container. Try to slip it out by turning the container on its side and gently pulling it away from the plant. Don't yank on the trunk. Give the sides and base of the container a few sharp raps if the tree doesn't slide out easily. Cut away the container if necessary; slit it from rim to base in several places, being careful that you don't cut through any big roots.

Take a hard look at the rootball. If the roots are matted or circling the rootball, pry or cut them loose. Don't worry about breaking small roots on the edge of the rootball.

Set the tree into the planting hole, lifting it with one hand on the trunk, one under the rootball. Check that the top of the rootball is at least 1 inch above the soil surface. Fill in around the rootball with the soil you dug from the hole, working it firmly between the roots and lifting the tree if necessary to keep it above soil level. Mound soil around the exposed rootball to cover the roots. Press the soil firmly around the tree.

Make a watering moat by building a 4-inch-high dike of soil around the planting hole. Water the tree thoroughly.

Place the birdbath to one side of the tree canopy—birds will love to settle on the lower branches of the tree and then alight into the birdbath once they've made sure the sights are clear. Rake the ground level, and moisten it if it's dry. Settle the birdbath firmly into the wet soil. Check the rim with the level to make sure that it's even. Fill the bowl with water to the very brim.

# FORMAL LINES AND
# EXCLAMATION POINTS

At Jack Chandler's garden in a small canyon in California's Napa Valley, the driveway turns through a tractor-red metal gate and arrives at an entrance court studded with poplar trees. The trees are set out geometrically, the lines of the trunks continuing the lines of the house out across the garden, settling the modern white architecture into the land, and establishing a beautiful transition—half architectural and half natural—between the living space and the wild canyon all around.

The yellow autumn leaves had almost all fallen and drifted away, the first time I visited, and the air smelled of the winter mold in the woods that would soon turn the leaves soggy. Wild mountain ash trees and maples were turning yellow beyond Jack's poplars, and long clear brown shadows of tree branches and trunks stretched across the gravel and white walls. The spirit of the natural landscape drifted everywhere through the garden, as if an echo had gone out to the canyon and back came patterns from nature across the treetops in the wind.

There's a cathedral peace in places bounded by repeating tree trunks and canopies soaring one after another interlaced into the sky. You feel impelled to walk the aisles, between the living columns, the sun on your back, and then on your cheeks as you turn, studying the season or the shape of a leaf.

A formal avenue, a grove of trees set on the square, or pairs and triangles of trees placed symmetrically like sentinels, or exclamation points, give the garden good bones. The straight lines sit especially well next to the house or at an entrance. Out in the thick of the garden, among the billowing loose forms of flowers and vines and vegetable plots, a straight line provides a little order, a peaceful place where the eye can rest.

# WEEPING HIGAN CHERRY ALLÉE

There's winter moisture still in the slats of the bench, so you walk on, meditatively, to and fro along the path, passing tree trunk after tree trunk, feet in the crisscrossing shadows of branches, head in the cherry blossom clouds. The air smells of boxwood and the mossy places in the gravel where damp has dripped from the trees. Fragile early spring sunshine bounces off the blossoms, striking warm against your face.

Under the lilting cherry trees, white Thalia daffodils and bluebells nod in the breeze. Eventually, showers bring down the cherry blossoms, which settle in soft, wet, pink pads on the paths and hedge tops. The last flowers speckle the crowns of the trees. Then the leaves come quickly, and the allée turns sheltered and green, a refuge from the summer sun.

# HOW TO DO IT ⋘

These single-flowered weeping Higan cherry trees (*Prunus subhirtella* 'Pendula') sit in a geometric grid, six trees in three pairs facing each other across the path. The trees are 10 years old, top-grafted at 5½ feet. They're as broad as they are tall, approximately 12 feet, and eventually they'll meet across the path.

Other species of flowering cherry are available, including white or pink double-flowering types. Be sure to choose a wide-spreading variety to make a tunnel of blossom. Buy from a reputable tree supplier. If one of the trees is mislabeled and you must replant, the set will never be even in growth.

The path is 6 feet wide, the bench 4 feet wide. Below the trees are hundreds of daffodil and bluebell bulbs and boxwood hedges. (The allée can be set up on lawn if you like, without the path, and with a water bowl on a pedestal instead of the bench as a destination.)

Mark the locations for the trees. Place the first pair 10 feet from the end of the garden, and 15 feet apart from trunk to trunk across the path (if your path is 6 feet wide, that will be 4½ feet from the path edge). Place the next pair 12 feet from the first. To make sure you're getting the rows straight, measure the distance from each tree trunk to the path; it must be the same as for the first pair. Set out the last pair of trees, 12 feet from the second pair, and, again, check the distance to the path.

Water each tree in its container. (If your trees are not in containers, see the instructions for planting bare-root and b&b trees, on pages 34 and 35.)

Dig the first planting hole. Make it three times as wide but not quite as deep as the container. The tree will grow better if the top of its rootball sits 1 inch above the surrounding soil (3 inches above if your soil doesn't drain well). Leaving a plateau of firm soil for the tree to sit on, dig 2 inches deeper around the edges of the hole so that the roots can grow down into loose soil. Loosen the soil around the sides of the hole to help the roots penetrate laterally.

Remove the tree from its container. Try to slip it out by turning the container on its side and gently pulling it away from the plant. Don't yank on the trunk. Give the sides and base of the container a few sharp raps if the tree doesn't slide out easily. Cut away the container if necessary; slit it from rim to base in several places, being careful that you don't cut through any big roots.

Take a hard look at the rootball. If the roots are matted or circling the rootball, pry or cut them loose. Don't worry about breaking small roots on the edge of the rootball.

Moderately expensive
Moderately easy
Location: Full sun
Soil: Well drained
Tree hardiness: Zones 5–8

## Tools
Measuring tape
Hose or watering can
Straight-edged spade
Trowel
Sharp knife

## Ingredients
6 flowering cherry trees (*Prunus* spp.), grafted at 5–6 feet or higher, broad-spreading habit
Boxwood (*Buxus* spp.), 4 plants per yard of path edge
300 or 600 bluebell bulbs (*Scilla*)
100 or 200 'Thalia' daffodil bulbs (*Narcissus triandrus* 'Thalia')

## Maintenance
Water trees and boxwood regularly until established, then moderately
Keep soil moist while bulbs are in bloom
Prune trees very lightly in winter to remove tangled and weak branches
Trim boxwood twice a year
Remove bulb foliage only when it has died back

Set the tree into the planting hole, lifting it with one hand on the trunk, one under the rootball. Check that the top of the rootball is at least 1 inch above the soil surface. Fill in around the rootball with the soil you dug from the hole, working it firmly between the roots and lifting the tree if necessary to keep it above soil level. Mound soil around the exposed rootball to cover the roots. Press the soil firmly around the tree.

Make a watering moat by building a 4-inch-high dike of soil around the planting hole. Water the tree thoroughly. Plant the other trees.

Plant the boxwood in the same manner, but don't worry about making a plateau in the planting hole, and set the rootballs just ½ inch above soil level. Space the plants 9 inches apart, 6 inches from the path edge.

Plant the bluebells around the tree trunks. Dig a trench 6 inches deep and 18 inches wide around each tree, beyond the rootball, and scatter 50 bluebell bulbs into the trench (or 100 bulbs, for a big show right from the first year). Cover the bulbs with soil, firm the soil, and water generously. Plant the daffodils in similar trenches in drifts between the trees, 25 or 50 bulbs per drift.

# GOLD PATH TURNER

These two golden American smoke trees lure people into the garden during fall. Soft mounds of blue-green rue shine with raindrops from last night's storm. The sedums have turned coarse copper-rose and are so heavy with seed and water that the stems have bent to the ground in places, revealing nests of new gray-green buds in the plant crowns. The wind has lifted up the skirts of the grasses, and brown bigleaf maple leaves blown in from another part of the garden are trapped, like lost kites, in the folds.

Brilliant yellow leaves from the trees glisten on the bank; some years they're orange or scarlet. The air smells sweetly soggy, fresh, and clean. Now that you're out, you're happy to walk on, toward other trees at other path corners— purple-stemmed yellowwood, white-and-raspberry-berried sorbus, yellow-orange cutleaf vine maple, pink-and-green dogwood—all around the richly colored, flowerless fall garden.

## HOW TO DO IT ◄◄◄

These two multi-trunked American smoke trees (*Cotinus obovatus*) are 6 or 7 years old. They may grow to 15 or 20 feet tall. In early summer, puffs of showy "smoke" surround the tiny flowers. Rue and sedum plants are set asymmetrically along the path. A pair of grasses at the path corner tunnels the view toward the trees.

Mark the locations for the trees. Place them 5 feet apart at the corner of the path.

Water each tree in its container. (If your trees are not in containers, see the instructions for planting bare-root and b&b trees, on pages 34 and 35.)

Dig the first planting hole. Make it three times as wide but not quite as deep as the container. The tree will grow better if the top of its rootball sits 1 inch above the surrounding soil (3 inches above if your soil doesn't drain well). Leaving a plateau of firm soil for the tree to sit on, dig 2 inches deeper around the edges of the hole so that the roots can grow down into loose soil. Loosen the soil around the sides of the hole to help the roots penetrate laterally.

Remove the tree from its container. Try to slip it out by turning the container on its side and gently pulling it away from the plant. Don't yank on the trunk. Give the sides and base of the container a few sharp raps if the tree doesn't slide out easily. Cut away the container if necessary; slit it from rim to base in several places, being careful that you don't cut through any big roots.

Take a hard look at the rootball. If the roots are matted or circling the rootball, pry or cut them loose. Don't worry about breaking small roots on the edge of the rootball.

Set the tree into the planting hole, lifting it with one hand on the trunk, one under the rootball. Check that the top of the rootball is at least 1 inch above the soil surface. Fill in around the rootball with the soil you dug from the hole, working it firmly between the roots and lifting the tree if necessary to keep it above soil level. Mound soil around the exposed rootball to cover the roots. Press the soil firmly around the tree.

Make a watering moat by building a 4-inch-high dike of soil around the planting hole. Water the tree thoroughly. Plant the second tree.

Plant the rue, sedums, and grasses in the same manner, but don't worry about making a plateau in the planting hole, and set the rootballs just ½ inch above soil level. Space the rue 1 to 3 feet apart, in clumps of one to seven plants, two or three clumps on each side of the path, in a rhythmic, staggered

---

Inexpensive
Easy
Location: Full sun or partial shade; wind tolerated
Soil: Most kinds, including clay, alkaline, and dry soils
Tree hardiness: Zones 5–8

**Tools**
Measuring tape
Hose or watering can
Straight-edged spade
Trowel
Sharp knife

**Ingredients**
2 multi-trunked American smoke trees (*Cotinus obovatus*)
Rue (*Ruta graveolens* 'Jackman's Blue'), at least 4 groups of 1 to 7 plants
Sedum (*Sedum telephium* 'Autumn Joy'), at least 3 groups of 1 to 7 plants
2 grasses (*Miscanthus sinensis* 'Yaku Jima')

**Maintenance**
Water tree and perennials regularly until established, then moderately
Keep soil moist while rue and sedum plants are in bloom
Fertilize rue and sedum plants in spring and midsummer
Cut back grasses to ground before growth starts in spring

pattern either side of the path. Plant the sedum in groups of one to seven also, 2 to 3 feet apart, in a similar staggered pattern along the path. Just before the corner, plant one grass on each side of the path, set back 3 feet from the path edge.

# LEMON-SCENTED GUMS,
## PINK GAZANIAS

At this garden entrance, shadows of
the lemon-scented gum trees wobble
against the wall with the motions of
the breeze—a gust and great movement,
then a whisper and gentle bobbing. The
wind sighs through the surrounding
woods in the same bursts and siftings,
and the rhythm echoes in the sounds of
the waves, rolling in and then receding
on a beach nearby.

Pausing, to catch more of these wild
murmurings, your eye might alight on
a convivial play of pinks by the wall.
Old eucalyptus leaves, crescents of
faded rose, rest among the buffy-pink
gazanias. The pinks are pale, blushing,
and dark, the same hues as the pinks
in the peeling tree bark. There's a corre-
spondence of green-grays here too—and
in the centers of the flowers and on the
inside of the bark a perfectly matched
natural gold.

**HOW TO DO IT** ⋘ These lemon-scented gums *(Eucalyptus citriodora)* are 4 years old. They are very fast growing and may reach 75 feet—imagine spectacularly tall, threadlike pale poles—but the tops will remain slender and graceful if you prune the trees carefully when they are young. Start with small healthy trees; they will grow much faster than large specimens that have grown too long in their containers.

Mark the locations for the trees. Place them 4 feet apart and at least 2 feet from a wall or fence.

Water each tree in its container. (If your trees are not in containers, see the instructions for planting bare-root and b&b trees, on pages 34 and 35.)

Dig the first planting hole. Make it three times as wide but not quite as deep as the container. The tree will grow better if the top of its rootball sits 1 inch above the surrounding soil (3 inches above if your soil doesn't drain well). Leaving a plateau of firm soil for the tree to sit on, dig 2 inches deeper around the edges of the hole so that the roots can grow down into loose soil. Loosen the soil around the sides of the hole to help the roots penetrate laterally.

Remove the tree from its container. Try to slip it out by turning the container on its side and gently pulling it away from the plant. Don't yank on the trunk. Give the sides and base of the container a few sharp raps if the tree doesn't slide out easily. Cut away the container if necessary; slit it from rim to base in several places, being careful that you don't cut through any big roots.

Take a hard look at the rootball. If the roots are matted or circling the rootball, pry or cut them loose. Don't worry about breaking small roots on the edge of the rootball.

Set the tree into the planting hole, lifting it with one hand on the trunk, one under the rootball. Check that the top of the rootball is at least 1 inch above the soil surface. Fill in around the rootball with the soil you dug from the hole, working it firmly between the roots and lifting the tree if necessary to keep it above soil level. Mound soil around the exposed rootball to cover the roots. Press the soil firmly around the tree.

Make a watering moat by building a 4-inch-high dike of soil around the planting hole. Water the tree thoroughly. Plant the second tree.

Stake each tree: Hammer a stake into the ground 1 foot from the trunk, and another on the other side of the tree, again 1 foot from the trunk. Tie the tree to the stakes about 4 feet from the ground, using two lengths of flexible

Inexpensive
Moderately easy
Location: Full sun
Soil: Most kinds, including dry soils
Tree hardiness: Zones 9–10

**Tools**
Measuring tape
Hose or watering can
Straight-edged spade
Trowel
Sharp knife
4 tree stakes, or two-by-twos, each 7 feet long
4 plastic tree ties, each 4 feet long
Hammer or mallet

**Ingredients**
2 lemon-scented gums *(Eucalyptus citriodora)*
Pink gazanias, 16 per square yard of planting bed

**Maintenance**
Water trees regularly through first growing season, then occasionally
Water gazanias regularly until established, then occasionally
Check tree ties twice a year; loosen as necessary; remove stakes and ties after two years
Prune trees annually for first three or four years

tree tie and leaving the ties on the loose side, so that the tree moves a little in the wind, gaining strength but prevented from falling.

Plant the gazania plants in the same manner as the trees, but don't worry about making a plateau in the planting hole, and set the rootballs just ½ inch above soil level. Space them 9 inches apart.

Shorten and thin the long slender tree branches every year for three or four years, so that the trees grow stronger. If they are top-heavy, they will rock and tilt. Because these trees grow so quickly, you will need to hire a professional with tree-pruning equipment once the trees outgrow your ladders.

# SNOWDRIFT CRABAPPLES, AUTUMN ROTS

The main walk in Virginia Israelit's garden descends across luxuriously scalloped lawn terraces under an allée of Snowdrift crabapples. It's such a lavish sweep, walking here feels like dancing: you glide back and forth on the soft grass between the planting beds, which swing along under the trees, then waltz down two steps, into shadow and out again into sunshine.

The trees are clouds of white blossoms in spring, but the most majestic moments arrive in fall. Then the leaves turn honey yellow, the crabapples ripen to orange-scarlet, the hostas collapse into hollows of lush brown rot, the stems of the Japanese forest grasses snap, the iris seedpods crack open to reveal chests of scarlet seeds. As the winter cold bites, the garden closes down colorfully and quietly until all that remains are hundreds of ripe apples on bare winter branches.

# HOW TO DO IT ⋘

These Snowdrift crabapple trees (*Malus* 'Snowdrift') sit in a geometric grid, six trees in three pairs facing each other across the allée. The trees are 10 years old, approximately 12 feet tall, and equally broad. They will meet each other across the allée eventually.

Other varieties of flowering crabapples are available, including ones with red or pink flowers, and double flowering types; the apples range from yellow to purple. Snowdrift has a long flowering season, its apples are also long lasting, and it has good disease resistance. Be sure to choose a round or widespreading variety to make a tunnel of foliage, and avoid all but the most disease-resistant varieties. Buy from a reputable tree supplier. If one of the trees is mislabeled and you must replant, the set will never be even in growth.

The slightly sloping, scalloped terraces are 10 to 20 feet wide and 12 feet deep, separated by pairs of stone steps. Have a contractor or landscape architect build the terraces and steps for you unless you're comfortable doing such work, or, to make a less expensive variation, create the allée on flat ground, in gravel instead of lawn if you like, and mark the points between the scallops with pots instead of steps.

Below the trees are irises, clumps of Japanese forest grass, ferns, hostas, astilbes, and feverfews.

Mark the locations for the trees. Place them 2 feet from the foot of the steps and 3 feet from the lawn edge. The trunks are 18 feet apart, measuring across the allée, and 12 feet apart within the rows.

Water each tree in its container. (If your trees are not in containers, see the instructions for planting bare-root and b&b trees, on pages 34 and 35.)

Dig the first planting hole. Make it three times as wide but not quite as deep as the container. The tree will grow better if the top of its rootball sits 1 inch above the surrounding soil (3 inches above if your soil doesn't drain well). Leaving a plateau of firm soil for the tree to sit on, dig 2 inches deeper around the edges of the hole so that the roots can grow down into loose soil. Loosen the soil around the sides of the hole to help the roots penetrate laterally.

Remove the tree from its container. Try to slip it out by turning the container on its side and gently pulling it away from the plant. Don't yank on the trunk. Give the sides and base of the container a few sharp raps if the tree doesn't slide out easily. Cut away the container if necessary; slit it from rim to base in several places, being careful that you don't cut through any big roots.

Moderately expensive
Moderately easy
Location: Full sun
Soil: Most well-drained types
Tree hardiness: Zones 4–8

**Tools**
Measuring tape
Hose or watering can
Straight-edged spade
Trowel
Sharp knife

**Ingredients**
6 Snowdrift crabapples (*Malus* 'Snowdrift'), or similar variety
6 Japanese forest grasses (*Hakonechloa macra* 'Aureola')
18 of each of the following: irises (*Iris pseudocorus variegatus*), ferns, hostas, astilbes, feverfews (*Chrysanthemum parthenium* 'Aureum')

**Maintenance**
Water trees and plants regularly
Prune trees in winter to remove tangled and weak branches
Remove suckers from the bases of the tree trunks in summer

Take a hard look at the rootball. If the roots are matted or circling the rootball, pry or cut them loose. Don't worry about breaking small roots on the edge of the rootball.

Set the tree into the planting hole, lifting it with one hand on the trunk, one under the rootball. Check that the top of the rootball is at least 1 inch above the soil surface. Fill in around the rootball with the soil you dug from the hole, working it firmly between the roots and lifting the tree if necessary to keep it above soil level. Mound soil around the exposed rootball to cover the roots. Press the soil firmly around the tree.

Make a watering moat by building a 4-inch-high dike of soil around the planting hole. Water the tree thoroughly. Plant the other trees.

Plant a Japanese forest grass beneath each tree, close to the foot of the steps and 18 inches from the lawn edge. These pairs of showy, gold-striped, bamboo-like grasses at the end of each terrace anchor the design. Make the rest of the planting informal: Plant an edging of hostas next to the grass on one side, astilbes or ferns or irises on the other side. For a good rhythm, plant in clumps of three; single plants will make the beds look spotty and restless.

# ANTIQUE APPLE HEDGE, MEDIEVAL FAVAS

*When the sun emerges after a rain shower, bumblebees start to drone through the fava beans and apple trees at the bottom of the garden. The petals of the apple are tissue veined with pink, and they smell of rain. The fava blossoms, parchment-white with black throats, smell so headily sweet that young women in medieval times were reputedly locked indoors while the favas bloomed.*

*When the sap has risen fully and the apple hedge is in leaf, the chives at the bases of the trunks will bloom and seed in pungent purple globes. Later, at the end of summer, the air will fill with smells of ripening fruit and harvest.*

# HOW TO DO IT ‹‹‹

This loosely espaliered dwarf apple tree (*Malus* 'Cox's Orange Pippin') is 10 years old. It is part of an apple tree hedge with interweaving branches, sometimes called a Belgian fence, that surrounds a square herb garden. The trees need pruning in summer and winter to keep them fruiting well and confined to the trellis, but the pruning is not difficult.

Buy dwarf trees (trees grafted onto dwarf rootstocks) that are 1 year old, so that you can train them; they are called *whips,* and they look like sticks. Specialist fruit tree growers offer a selection of cultivars; choose any you like, as long as it isn't a vigorous variety. Most varieties need other apple varieties nearby to pollinate them—hence, the benefit of an apple hedge, each tree a suitable pollinator for the others (the supplier will advise you about suitable pollinators). Apple trees usually require a certain amount of winter chill; in mild-winter climates, only a few varieties grow well.

The trellis is built of heartwood redwood, although pressure-treated wood or heartwood cedar would do just as well. It has four-by-four posts, two-by-four beams at top and bottom, and one-by-two diagonal crossbeams. Each section (one section per tree) is 6 feet wide and 4½ feet high. The posts are sunk in concrete, for stability. Unless you're comfortable building fences, you should have a contractor build the trellis. Or grow your apple hedge against an existing fence or wall, tying the branches to tight diagonal wires, bolted 4 to 6 inches away from the upright structure.

Mark the location for the trees. Place them 6 inches in front of the trellis, 6 feet apart, at the center of the trellis frames. Water each tree in its container. (If your trees are not in containers, see the instructions for planting bare-root and b&b trees, on pages 34 and 35.)

Dig the first planting hole. Make it three times as wide but not quite as deep as the container. The tree will grow better if the top of its rootball sits 1 inch above the surrounding soil (3 inches above if your soil doesn't drain well). Leaving a plateau of firm soil for the tree to sit on, dig 2 inches deeper around the edges of the hole so that the roots can grow down into loose soil. Loosen the soil around the sides of the hole to help the roots penetrate laterally.

Remove the tree from its container. Try to slip it out by turning the container on its side and gently pulling it away from the plant. Don't yank on the trunk. Give the sides and base of the container a few sharp raps if the tree doesn't slide out easily. Cut away the container if necessary; slit it from rim to base in several places, being careful that you don't cut through any big roots.

Moderately inexpensive
Moderately easy
Location: Full sun
Soil: Well drained, fertile
Tree hardiness: Zones 2–9

**Tools**
Measuring tape
Hose or watering can
Straight-edged spade
Trowel
Sharp knife
Bucket, for diluting paint
White latex (water-based) paint
Paintbrush
Sharp pruners
Plant ties or soft string

**Ingredients**
Dwarf apple trees, 1-year-old whips, any nonvigorous varieties that pollinate one another, 1 per 6-foot section of trellis
Trellis (see text)
Fava bean seeds, 1 packet
Chives, 20 plants per 6-foot section of trellis

**Maintenance**
Water trees, favas, and chives regularly until established
Keep soil around trees moist from apple blossom time until harvest
Water favas moderately until harvest
Apply mulch around trees each spring (optional); don't fertilize
Prune trees in summer and winter (see text)
Sow new favas each year
In fall, trim chives close to base; they will regrow in spring

Take a hard look at the rootball. If the roots are matted or circling the rootball, pry or cut them loose. Don't worry about breaking small roots on the edge of the rootball.

Set the tree into the planting hole, lifting it with one hand on the trunk, one under the rootball. Check that the top of the rootball is at least 1 inch above the soil surface. Fill in around the rootball with the soil you dug from the hole, working it firmly between the roots and lifting the tree if necessary to keep it above soil level. Mound soil around the exposed rootball to cover the roots. Press the soil firmly around the tree.

Make a watering moat by building a 4-inch-high dike of soil around the planting hole. Water the tree thoroughly. Plant the other trees. In hot summer climates, whitewash the tree trunks before their first summer, to prevent sunburn. Dilute the paint with water, and brush it on. Start formative pruning of the trees right away.

*First pruning:* After planting, immediately cut back the stem to within 15 or 18 inches of the ground. Make the cut above two buds facing in opposite directions, if possible. Use very sharp pruners, and slant the cut, so that moisture will roll off it and not seep into the wood. The high side of the cut should be ¼ to ½ inch above the highest bud. In spring, the two buds and maybe some others will produce branches off the short trunk. Let these branches grow freely until fall.

*Second pruning:* In fall, lower the two opposite-facing branches and tie them loosely to the diagonal beams of the trellis with plant ties or soft string. (These are your main branches, which you'll train along the diagonal beams for the next few years.) To encourage them to grow, cut these two branches back by one third, to just above a bud, angling the cuts as you did in the first pruning. If other branches have grown from the trunk, cut them right back to three buds, so they won't compete with the main branches. Let the trees grow freely until next summer.

*Third pruning:* In summer, you'll see vertical side shoots now growing off your main branches. Leave the tips of the main branches alone, but prune back the side shoots to the lowest cluster of three leaves. These stubs will become fruiting spurs, and you want as many of them as possible.

*Fall prunings:* Every fall, prune the new extension growth on the main branches by one third and re-tie the branches to the diagonal beams (note how the branches cross the posts onto the diagonal beam in the next section of trellis). When the main branches reach the edges of the trellis, remove the new growth entirely. Remove tangled or diseased twigs.

*Summer prunings:* Every summer, prune back most of the side shoots to form fruiting spurs, but now that the main branches are growing strongly you can let a few side shoots grow into the center, to fill the spaces between cross-beams. When those produce side shoots, prune them back to the lowest cluster of three leaves, to make more fruiting spurs.

In early spring (or in fall, if your winter climate is mild), sow the fava beans in a nearby bed. Place the seeds 1 inch deep, 4 inches apart, in rows 2 feet apart. When the seedlings emerge, thin them to 8 inches apart. In midspring, plant the chives 9 inches apart in a 2-foot-wide bed beneath the apple trees.

# TRIANGLE OF TWISTERS

The Italian cypresses have shinnied up through a jungle of rose briars and kiwi vines, coiffure winning out against chaos. The trees go up and up and up, surging from the undergrowth with their ziggy haircuts, past the points where the vines sag from gravity, pushing the garden into the sky.

From every stopping place in Marcia Donahue's garden, the cypresses soar over the tangle of flowers and branches. They appear through a palm tree from one direction, through a tree sporting blue bottles in another, generating escape routes from the small, plant-packed city garden to the universe beyond.

The trees are also beacons. If you make your way to them through the jungle, you'll come upon a clearing with a quiet pond.

# HOW TO DO IT ⋘

These three Italian cypresses (*Cupressus sempervirens* 'Stricta') are about 15 feet tall and 15 years old, but they were topped at 12 years, when they threatened to grow beyond the reach of the pruning ladder. Untopped, they might have grown to 60 feet. The trees were pruned into spirals when they were young and now are trimmed two or three times a year.

Mark the locations for the trees. Perhaps align them with an entrance to the house or with a bench in the garden, or mark a special site with them as Marcia has done. Their roots are not invasive or greedy, so you can place them among other plantings, and they seem to soar more coming up through thickets of roses and shrubs than standing alone as sentinels. Place the trees 3 feet apart.

Water each tree in its container. (If your trees are not in containers, see the instructions for planting bare-root and b&b trees, on pages 34 and 35.)

Dig the first planting hole. Make it three times as wide but not quite as deep as the container. The tree will grow better if the top of its rootball sits 1 inch above the surrounding soil (3 inches above if your soil doesn't drain well). Leaving a plateau of firm soil for the tree to sit on, dig 2 inches deeper around the edges of the hole so that the roots can grow down into loose soil. Loosen the soil around the sides of the hole to help the roots penetrate laterally.

Remove the tree from its container. Try to slip it out by turning the container on its side and gently pulling it away from the plant. Don't yank on the trunk. Give the sides and base of the container a few sharp raps if the tree doesn't slide out easily. Cut away the container if necessary; slit it from rim to base in several places, being careful that you don't cut through any big roots.

Take a hard look at the rootball. If the roots are matted or circling the rootball, pry or cut them loose. Don't worry about breaking small roots on the edge of the rootball.

Set the tree into the planting hole, lifting it with one hand on the trunk, one under the rootball. Check that the top of the rootball is at least 1 inch above the soil surface. Fill in around the rootball with the soil you dug from the hole, working it firmly between the roots and lifting the tree if necessary to keep it above soil level. Mound soil around the exposed rootball to cover the roots. Press the soil firmly around the tree.

Make a watering moat by building a 4-inch-high dike of soil around the planting hole. Water the tree thoroughly. Plant the other trees.

Allow the trees to grow naturally for a year. When they are well estab-

Inexpensive
Moderately easy
Location: Full sun or light shade
Soil: Most kinds, except soggy or very dry soils
Tree hardiness: Zones 8–10

**Tools**
Measuring tape
Hose or watering can
Straight-edged spade
Trowel
Sharp knife
Pruning shears

**Ingredients**
3 Italian cypresses (*Cupressus sempervirens* 'Stricta'), about 3 feet tall

**Maintenance**
Water trees regularly until established, then moderately
Trim ribbons of foliage two or three times a year

lished, shave them into twisters: Identify a ribbon of foliage about 4 inches wide, and remove the foliage to either side of it, cutting it out completely, right back to the trunk, no stubble. Don't fret about making the ribbon twist regularly around the trunk. Marcia made hers purposely wonky and wishes they were even wonkier. An even twist will look static, a wonky one full of movement. So settle courageously into wonkiness from the start; once you have shaved the foliage back to the trunk, it will not regrow.

When you have carved the twists, trim their foliage back to within 6 inches of the trunk to keep it from getting shaggy. Trim again every four to six months so that the foliage stays tight to the trunk.

# OLIVE ORCHARD
# WITH LAVENDER

*A warm-colored Mediterranean-style house sits back from a country road behind an orchard of olive trees and lavender. The soft gray-green foliage billows over a floor of sandy decomposed granite, the same surface that is used for boules courts in France. Through the loose treetops, the garden skyline is punctuated by trim spires of black-green cypress trees, another feature common in the Mediterranean countryside.*

*On a warm morning in late spring, pale-green shoots have sprouted among the willowy olive leaves and are forming flower buds. Soon they will break open into sprays of tiny fragrant white blooms. The older foliage, which has light-gray undersides, flashes silver as the trees blow in the wind.*

*The lavenders are becoming fuzzy mounds of fresh mauve flowers. When the breeze drops, you can hear honeybees hazing them for food.*

# HOW TO DO IT ⋘

These multi-trunked olive trees *(Olea europaea)* and Spanish lavender bushes are 7 years old. The olives will grow to about 25 or 30 feet tall and develop knotty, picturesque trunks. Be sure to buy multi-trunked trees, if possible, to have the greatest amount of trunk. Choose a nonfruiting variety if you do not want the olive fruits (they are messy if they drop into grass or onto flagstone paving). The lavender beds were originally also planted with Emerald Carpet manzanita, a low-mounding bright-green ground cover.

In cold climates, substitute apple or pear trees for the olives and honeysuckle for the lavender. Any kind of lavender, including English, the most fragrant kind, may be grown instead of Spanish lavender. French lavender has by far the longest flowering season; in mild climates, it blooms intermittently all year.

The orchard is set in decomposed granite (d.g.), but it could be planted into grass or bare soil. If you decide to lay the d.g., follow the directions at the end of the recipe. Because of the scale of the project and the weight of the materials, you might consider hiring a contractor to do the work.

Mark out the orchard boundary and rows with stakes and twine. You'll need an area about 24 yards wide to fit three rows of trees and four rows of lavender, and 18 yards deep to fit three trees in each corridor.

Standing on the long (24-yard) side of the orchard, mark out a lavender bed 3 yards wide. Alongside it, mark out a corridor 4 yards wide for trees. Mark out another lavender bed and another corridor for trees twice more, and then one more bed of lavender. (If you are laying d.g., lay it now; see the directions at the end of the recipe.)

Mark the locations for the trees; place them in the centers of the corridors, 6 yards apart, the first one 3 yards in from the 24-yard edge of the orchard.

Water each tree in its container. (If your trees are not in containers, see the instructions for planting bare-root and b&b trees, on pages 34 and 35.)

Dig the first planting hole. Make it three times as wide but not quite as deep as the container. The tree will grow better if the top of its rootball sits 1 inch above the surrounding soil (3 inches above if your soil doesn't drain well). Leaving a plateau of firm soil for the tree to sit on, dig 2 inches deeper around the edges of the hole so that the roots can grow down into loose soil. Loosen the soil around the sides of the hole to help the roots penetrate laterally.

Moderately expensive
Moderately easy
Location: Full sun, hot dry summers
Soil: Most well-drained kinds
Tree hardiness: Zones 9–10

## Tools
Measuring tape
Stakes and twine
Hose or watering can
Straight-edged spade
Trowel
Sharp knife

## For the d.g. corridors
Rake
Hammer
Saw
Shovel, for spreading materials
Hand-held tamper or water-fillable roller

## Ingredients
9 olive trees *(Olea europaea)*
108 Spanish lavender plants *(Lavandula stoechas)*, 1 per 2 feet of planting row
88 manzanitas *(Arctostaphylos* 'Emerald Carpet') (optional), 2 per 5 feet of planting row

## For the d.g. corridors
Redwood, heartwood cedar, or treated wood two-by-sixes, for edging, 132 yards
100 stake two-by-twos, 18 inches long, 1 per 4 feet of tree corridor perimeter, and 3-inch nails
Crushed rock, ¾-inch, 13 cubic yards
Decomposed granite (d.g.), ¼-inch minus, 13 cubic yards

## Maintenance
Water trees, lavender, and manzanitas regularly until established, then moderately
Cut back lavender after flowering, to keep plants neat
Harvest olives in fall
Prune olive trees in fall: pull off (don't cut) suckers at base of tree; cut out some branches, if necessary, to keep centers of trees open

Remove the tree from its container. Try to slip it out by turning the container on its side and gently pulling it away from the plant. Don't yank on the trunk. Give the sides and base of the container a few sharp raps if the tree doesn't slide out easily. Cut away the container if necessary; slit it from rim to base in several places, being careful that you don't cut through any big roots.

Take a hard look at the rootball. If the roots are matted or circling the rootball, pry or cut them loose. Don't worry about breaking small roots on the edge of the rootball.

Set the tree into the planting hole, lifting it with one hand on the trunk, one under the rootball. Check that the top of the rootball is at least 1 inch above the soil surface. Fill in around the rootball with the soil you dug from the hole, working it firmly between the roots and lifting the tree if necessary to keep it above soil level. Mound soil around the exposed rootball to cover the roots. Press the soil firmly around the tree.

Make a watering moat by building a 4-inch-high dike of soil around the planting hole. Water the tree thoroughly. Plant the other trees.

Plant the manzanitas (optional) and the lavender bushes in the same manner, but don't worry about making a plateau in the planting hole, and set the rootballs just ½ inch above soil level. Space the lavenders 2 feet apart down the center of the beds. Plant the manzanitas in two rows, one on each side of the lavenders, spaced 5 feet apart.

*To lay the decomposed granite* (2 inches of d.g., laid on a foundation of 2 inches of crushed rock, and edged with wood two-by-sixes):

Before planting, clear any weeds, and rake the ground level. Dig a 4-inch-deep trench the length and width of the tree corridors. Firm the bottom of the trench if you've disturbed the soil while digging.

For the wood edging, drive the stake two-by-twos into the sides of the trench, outside the twine, at intervals of 4 feet. Position the edging two-by-sixes in the trench, narrow side up, so that they protrude above the top of the trench, and nail them to the stakes, holding or wedging the stakes firmly upright during the hammering. Firm the soil against the outside of the edging. Saw off any protruding stakes flush with the edging.

Plant the trees now. Make sure that the tops of the rootballs sit 5 inches above the bottom of the trench. Cover any protruding roots with soil. Don't bother making watering moats.

Spread a 2-inch layer of crushed rock into the bottom of the trench. Moisten it, and pack down the surface with the tamper or roller. Be careful not to scrape the trunks of the trees or damage the roots.

Spread a 2-inch layer of d.g. over the crushed rock. Mound a ½-inch layer of d.g. over the rootballs of the trees. Tamp or roll the finished surface thoroughly, again being careful around the trees.

Check that the trees sit higher than the surrounding d.g., so that water doesn't drain toward the tree trunks.

# NATURAL GROUPS

Trees left to their own devices form thickets and copses. Inside, among the trunks, lies a place of complete solitude. We feel a primeval sense of shelter and comfort there, enclosed in the greenery. Like caves and firesides, says landscape architect Rich Haag, natural tree places are "encoded into our DNA."

In nature, trees are often multi-trunked, sometimes because grazing animals have taken out the tips when the trees were knee-high. The forms are free and individual, full of chance and grace. For natural groups in the garden, choose a combination of single- and multi-trunked trees, and don't worry if the branching isn't symmetrical. If you plant them closely, they'll stretch and lean naturally toward the light.

The most beautiful natural groves are a simple expression of one main theme—a maple wood, a birch grove, a cherry orchard. Settle on a single species of tree and an understory of one kind of grass or a shade-loving shrub or vine. The repetition of leaf and flower and arching branch throughout the garden makes a restful, quiet stability.

To invite people into the darkness under the trees, light the way with a colorful shrub or a procession of arches, shining tree trunks, and glittering bottles along the path. In dank winter climates, avoid planting trees close to the house. Set up your copse at the end of the garden, or choose deciduous trees, and make clearings at the house entrance and around the windows so that the light pools there and streams indoors.

# MAPLE GROVE

*Before the morning mist has left the lawn, the lightly burnt orange and cherry-red leaves in this small maple grove have picked up the glow of the light in the sky. Dew glistens in the foliage, and the dark pencil-thin branches rise on every breeze, mixing the treetops into a blur of soft autumnal color.*

*Walking through, you feel the lower branches quivering over the path. A burst of sunshine catches papery strips of cinnamon bark peeling from one of the trunks. On other trees, dainty scarlet winged seeds (samaras) spin among crimson leaves. A suspended water droplet mirrors a world wrapped in autumn maples—varicolored leaves cartwheeling over the ground, and forked branches dipping in waves and troughs under the brightening sky.*

HOW TO DO IT ◄◄◄ These maples are 15 to 25 feet tall, and virtually fully grown. Some are more than 20 years old. The grove has a unified, delicate look because most of the trees are cultivars of dainty Japanese maples, *Acer palmatum.* Up close, the colors of the bark, leaf bracts, and emerging leaves are beautifully diverse. The maple with cinnamon peeling bark is paperbark maple *(Acer griseum),* the one with scarlet samaras, *Acer palmatum* 'Osakazuki.' The grove also includes trident maples *(Acer buergerianum).*

Moss and grass cover the floor, with a few ferns among the tree trunks and a dirt path running through the middle. You could plant the grove in an existing lawn or even in a small courtyard, where the trees would vine nicely toward the light. Keep the ground below almost free of plantings, the better to display the fall leaves.

Buy multi-trunked trees if possible, or single-trunked trees with slanting trunks and an irregular, twisting habit. If you have the chance, buy locally, so that you can see the fall color in your area. Don't hesitate to buy unnamed seedling trees if they show lovely color; they will probably grow faster than the bred varieties. Avoid symmetrical, grafted specimen trees and those with finely dissected leaves or purple summer foliage, because they'll spoil the natural, woodland look of the grove.

Mark the locations for the trees. Space them irregularly, 8 to 12 feet apart. Leave a 12-foot-wide clearing through the middle, if you have enough space, for the joy of ambling there under branches arching gracefully into the light. Avoid forming a row from any angle.

Water each tree in its container. (If your trees are not in containers, see the instructions for planting bare-root and b&b trees, on pages 34 and 35.)

Dig the first planting hole. Make it three times as wide but not quite as deep as the container. The tree will grow better if the top of its rootball sits 1 inch above the surrounding soil (3 inches above if your soil doesn't drain well). Leaving a plateau of firm soil for the tree to sit on, dig 2 inches deeper around the edges of the hole so that the roots can grow down into loose soil. Loosen the soil around the sides of the hole to help the roots penetrate laterally.

Remove the tree from its container. Try to slip it out by turning the container on its side and gently pulling it away from the plant. Don't yank on the trunk. Give the sides and base of the container a few sharp raps if the tree doesn't slide out easily. Cut away the container if necessary;

Moderately inexpensive
Easy
Location: Shelter from wind; partial shade preferred
Soil: Rich, moist
Tree hardiness: Zones 6–8

**Tools**
Measuring tape
Hose or watering can
Straight-edged spade
Trowel
Sharp knife

**Ingredients**
5 to 9 maple trees, mostly *Acer palmatum* (see text)
6 to 9 native ferns

**Maintenance**
Water trees and ferns regularly until established, then moderately
During long dry periods, water every two weeks

slit it from rim to base in several places, being careful that you don't cut through any big roots.

Take a hard look at the rootball. If the roots are matted or circling the rootball, pry or cut them loose. Don't worry about breaking small roots on the edge of the rootball.

Set the tree into the planting hole, lifting it with one hand on the trunk, one under the rootball. Check that the top of the rootball is at least 1 inch above the soil surface. Fill in around the rootball with the soil you dug from the hole, working it firmly between the roots and lifting the tree if necessary to keep it above soil level. Mound soil around the exposed rootball to cover the roots. Press the soil firmly around the tree.

Make a watering moat by building a 4-inch-high dike of soil around the planting hole. Water the tree thoroughly. Plant the other trees.

Plant the ferns in the same manner, but don't worry about making a plateau in the planting hole, and set the rootballs just ½ inch above soil level. Place them in clumps of two or three at the foot of a few trees.

# CHITALPAS, GRAVEL WASH

A grass path runs along an isthmus between a pond and a dry gravel wash. In the wash, Mexican feather grasses, which have turned golden and soft early because of the dryness, dust the trunks of chitalpa trees. Thrifty, fast-growing relatives of the desert willow, these trees thrive in wind and sand, waiting months for rain.

In the dry summer months, instead of hunkering down and reserving their energies, the trees produce wave after wave of fragrant tropical-looking blossoms. The clusters of frilly white trumpets veined with purple lure birds. The white petals drift into the golden grasses.

When the first splashes of rain arrive, a sage aroma bursts from the salvia under the trees. Long bean pods begin to form on the tree branches; these will hang on after the willowy foliage drops onto the gravel and the wash is glazed by frost.

# HOW TO DO IT ◄◄◄

These 4-year-old chitalpas (*Chitalpa tashkentensis* 'Morning Cloud') are crosses between desert willow *(Chilopsis linearis)* and catalpa or Indian bean *(Catalpa bignonioides)*. They may grow to 25 feet. A few small boulders sit among the trees; their hard surfaces and weight contrast nicely with the feathery grasses and tree blossoms. Be sure to choose gravel that is similar in color to the boulders, as if formed from the same rock. If you can't maneuver the boulders easily, ask a friend to help, or see whether the supplier will position them.

Mark the outline of the wash, laying the twine along the ground. Make it about 15 feet long and 6 feet wide in the middle, tapering at one end (the high end if you are working on a slope) and forming a 9-foot-wide pool at the other. If there's a sweep in a line of shrubs or a lawn area nearby, have the banks of the wash swing with those lines; the repetition will exaggerate the sense of movement beautifully. The most natural place for a wash is in a low-lying part of the garden or tipping gently across a sloping lawn.

Remove 3 inches of soil from the wash, so that you can lay 2 inches of gravel and still have the wash be lower than the surrounding garden.

Mark the locations of the trees. Stagger them, 8 feet or so apart, through the wash, one toward the tapered end, two almost across from one another at the pool.

Before you plant the trees, place the boulders: one at the tapered end, anchoring that point; and the other two under the trees in the pool of the wash. Bury the bottom third of the boulders so that they'll seem to be part of the bedrock.

Water each tree in its container. (If your trees are not in containers, see the instructions for planting bare-root and b&b trees, on pages 34 and 35.)

Dig the first planting hole. Make it three times as wide but not quite as deep as the container. The tree will grow better if the top of its rootball sits 1½ inches above the soil inside the wash. Leaving a plateau of firm soil for the tree to sit on,

Moderately inexpensive
Moderately difficult
Location: Full sun; wind tolerated
Soil: Most kinds, including poor, dry ones
Tree hardiness: Zones 6–9

**Tools**

2 balls of twine and bundle of
    marking stakes
Measuring tape
Straight-edged spade
Hose or watering can
Trowel
Sharp knife
Rake
Shovel

**Ingredients**

3 chitalpas (*Chitalpa tashkentensis*
    'Morning Cloud')
3 small boulders
2 deer grasses *(Muhlenbergia rigens)*,
    or other evergreen grasses
6 Mexican feather grasses *(Stipa
    tenuissima)*
1 salvia *(Salvia clevelandii* 'Allen
    Chickering')
Tan gravel (or other color to match
    boulders), ¾-inch, approx. 15 cubic
    feet total, or 1½ cubic feet per
    square yard

**Maintenance**

Water trees, grasses, and salvia regularly
    until established, then only moderately
    or occasionally
Prune up lowest tree branches and thin
    branches, as necessary (see text)

dig 2 inches deeper around the edges of the hole so that the roots can grow down into loose soil. Loosen the soil around the sides of the hole to help the roots penetrate laterally.

Remove the tree from its container. Try to slip it out by turning the container on its side and gently pulling it away from the plant. Don't yank on the trunk. Give the sides and base of the container a few sharp raps if the tree doesn't slide out easily. Cut away the container if necessary; slit it from rim to base in several places, being careful that you don't cut through any big roots.

Take a hard look at the rootball. If the roots are matted or circling the rootball, pry or cut them loose. Don't worry about breaking small roots on the edge of the rootball.

Set the tree into the planting hole, lifting it with one hand on the trunk, one under the rootball. Check that the top of the rootball is at least 1½ inches above the soil surface. Fill in around the rootball with the soil you dug from the hole, working it firmly between the roots and lifting the tree if necessary to keep it above soil level. Mound soil around the exposed rootball to cover the roots. Press the soil firmly around the tree. Water the tree thoroughly. Plant the other trees.

Plant the grasses and salvia in the same manner, setting the tops of the rootballs 1½ inches above the soil level of the wash, but don't worry about making a plateau in the planting hole. Place the deer grasses, 3 feet apart, at the tapered end of the wash and the Mexican feather grasses, 4 feet apart, in the center of the wash, between the trees. Place the salvia at the pool end.

Rake the soil the length of the wash and firm any areas you've disturbed while digging. Spread the gravel 2 inches deep through the wash. Scatter a thin layer of gravel over the plant rootballs, just enough to hide the soil, being careful not to damage the trunks of the trees.

To prevent the trees from becoming shrubby, during the winter after the first growing season (or, if a tree isn't established and putting out strong new growth, wait another year), shorten the lowest tree branches. Remove them entirely the following year. Thin the trees each winter, as necessary, cutting side branches back to main branches, to reveal the pretty architecture of the smooth trunks.

# WOODLAND CLEARING,
# CABIN ENTRANCE

*Inside the garden gates, off the country road, the conifers have been thinned to let shafts of light fall 100 feet through the bottle-green darkness to the earth below. The scale is magnificent here—soaring treetops whistling with clean air, small fir cones on the quiet forest floor, and Lake Whatcom glinting silver beyond the straight trunks of the trees.*

*When the cabin comes into view through the dark forest, it lies in a pool of light, and the scale turns from majestic to welcoming. A copse of slender serviceberry trees, closer to human height, lights up the entrance with a flurry of profuse white flowers in spring. In fall, warm yellow-and-orange foliage waves over the rooflines, and the leaves float down to the doorstep, collecting around Olla Maiden wrapped in the warmth of the cabin and the woodland ferns.*

HOW TO DO IT ⋘ This grove of multi-trunked serviceberry tree-shrubs *(Amelanchier canadensis),* also called juneberry or shadbush, is 8 years old. The trees may grow to 20 feet. Small, sweet, edible black fruits follow the flowers. Kerria shrubs, green-stemmed with yellow pompom flowers in spring, grow beneath the serviceberry; elsewhere native ferns cover the garden floor. The porch garden area is approximately 15 by 20 feet.

Mark the locations for the trees. Cluster them 8 feet apart close to the porch, 10 feet apart farther out in the garden. Avoid forming a row from any angle.

Water each tree in its container. (If your trees are not in containers, see the instructions for planting bare-root and b&b trees, on pages 34 and 35.)

Dig the first planting hole. Make it three times as wide but not quite as deep as the container. The tree will grow better if the top of its rootball sits 1 inch above the surrounding soil (3 inches above if your soil doesn't drain well). Leaving a plateau of firm soil for the tree to sit on, dig 2 inches deeper around the edges of the hole so that the roots can grow down into loose soil. Loosen the soil around the sides of the hole to help the roots penetrate laterally.

Remove the tree from its container. Try to slip it out by turning the container on its side and gently pulling it away from the plant. Don't yank on the trunk. Give the sides and base of the container a few sharp raps if the tree doesn't slide out easily. Cut away the container if necessary; slit it from rim to base in several places, being careful that you don't cut through any big roots.

Take a hard look at the rootball. If the roots are matted or circling the rootball, pry or cut them loose. Don't worry about breaking small roots on the edge of the rootball.

Set the tree into the planting hole, lifting it with one hand on the trunk, one under the rootball. Check that the top of the rootball is at least 1 inch above the soil surface. Fill in around the rootball with the soil you dug from the hole, working it firmly between the roots and lifting the tree if necessary to keep it above soil level. Mound soil around the exposed rootball to cover the roots. Press the soil firmly around the tree.

Make a watering moat by building a 4-inch-high dike of soil around the planting hole. Water the tree thoroughly. Plant the other trees.

Plant the kerrias and ferns in the same manner, but don't worry about making a plateau in the planting hole, and set the rootballs just ½ inch above soil level. Space the kerrias irregularly, about 4 feet apart, and the ferns approximately 3 feet apart.

Moderately inexpensive
Easy
Location: Full sun or partial shade
Soil: Well drained, not alkaline or dry
Hardiness: Zones 4–9

**Tools**
Measuring tape
Hose or watering can
Straight-edged spade
Trowel
Sharp knife

**Ingredients**
8 serviceberry trees (*Amelanchier* spp.)
5 kerrias (*Kerria japonica*)
12 or so native ferns

**Maintenance**
Water trees and other plants regularly until established, then moderately
Remove suckers from trees, to prevent them from becoming shrubby
Prune kerrias heavily after flowering, cutting out branches that have bloomed

# MAPLES, MOSS, AND VARICOLORED DISANTHUS

One corner of this Victorian country house is nestled into cozy darkness. Western red cedars stand just a few yards from the walls, a shady black-green screen that catches and calms the wind from high over the roofline down to the garden floor.

In the quiet understory grow maples, their slender trunks forking and slanting around a mossy stone path. The branches touch the house windows and throw shadows across the wallpaper indoors, knitting the towering conifers lightly to the house in a web of pretty lines and leaves.

At the entrance to the dappled darkness, a remarkable shrub-tree, a relative of witch hazel, Disanthus cercidifolius, even lower than the maples, calls you in over the uneven stones. In early fall, its loose waves of joyously varicolored leaves—pink, yellow, green, wine red, purple—chase the chinks of light on the emerald moss and the golden sunlight warming the purple porch.

HOW TO DO IT ⋘ The maples (*Acer palmatum*) and disanthus are 7 years old; they are almost fully grown. Below the disanthus, on each side of the path are smooth hydrangeas, which signal the entrance to the path with huge round white flowers all through summer. The Western red cedars were planted by a former owner; before the maple planting, they towered darkly over the house, out of scale with the garden.

Mark the locations for the maples. Space them irregularly, 8 to 10 feet apart, at least 5 feet from the house. Place the disanthus at the entrance to the maple grove.

Water each tree in its container. (If your trees are not in containers, see the instructions for planting bare-root and b&b trees, on pages 34 and 35.)

Dig the first planting hole. Make it three times as wide but not quite as deep as the container. The tree will grow better if the top of its rootball sits 1 inch above the surrounding soil (3 inches above if your soil doesn't drain well). Leaving a plateau of firm soil for the tree to sit on, dig 2 inches deeper around the edges of the hole so that the roots can grow down into loose soil. Loosen the soil around the sides of the hole to help the roots penetrate laterally.

Remove the tree from its container. Try to slip it out by turning the container on its side and gently pulling it away from the plant. Don't yank on the trunk. Give the sides and base of the container a few sharp raps if the tree doesn't slide out easily. Cut away the container if necessary; slit it from rim to base in several places, being careful that you don't cut through any big roots.

Take a hard look at the rootball. If the roots are matted or circling the rootball, pry or cut them loose. Don't worry about breaking small roots on the edge of the rootball.

Set the tree into the planting hole, lifting it with one hand on the trunk, one under the rootball. Check that the top of the rootball is at least 1 inch above the soil surface. Fill in around the rootball with the soil you dug from the hole, working it firmly between the roots and lifting the tree if necessary to keep it above soil level. Mound soil around the exposed rootball to cover the roots. Press the soil firmly around the tree.

Make a watering moat by building a 4-inch-high dike of soil around the planting hole. Water the tree thoroughly. Plant the other trees.

Plant the disanthus and hydrangeas in the same manner, but don't worry about making a plateau in the planting hole, and set the rootballs just ½ inch above soil level.

Moderately inexpensive
Easy
Location: Shelter from wind; partial shade preferred
Soil: Rich, moist
Tree hardiness: Zones 6–8

**Tools**
Measuring tape
Hose or watering can
Straight-edged spade
Trowel
Sharp knife

**Ingredients**
5 maples (*Acer palmatum*)
1 disanthus (*Disanthus cercidifolius*)
2 smooth hydrangeas (*Hydrangea arborescens*)

**Maintenance**
Water trees and hydrangeas regularly until established, then moderately
During long dry periods, water every two weeks
Remove hydrangea flower stalks after flowering

# CALIFORNIA BAYS,
# BORROWED COUNTRYSIDE

Along a winding road through the hills to this house, the views are of bay trees with dry grasses and wild penstemons, bay trees and stables and horse manure, bay trees and the damp shade of mossy oak and stream. The pungent fragrance of the leaves, which so strongly marks this landscape as home, drifts into the house from the arrival court, where these two cultivated bay trees grow, their trunks splayed as if deer had stepped on them as seedlings.

The sculpture, Long Meadow, in front of the trees catches the patterns of leaf, flower, and cloud in this part of the world. The light traveling in the morning mist swells on the glass. At noon, branch shadows drum over the surface; and when the sun sinks over the hilltop, the last rays silhouette the grasses and lavender spikes.

# HOW TO DO IT ≪≪≪

These California bay trees (*Umbellularia cali-fornica*) are about 30 years old. They may grow to large trees eventually if not kept in check by pruning. Be sure to plant bays only if they exist in the landscape. Otherwise, substitute any well-behaved tree of reasonable size that grows in your local landscape.

Mark the locations for the trees. Place them 3 feet apart.

Water each tree in its container. (If your trees are not in containers, see the instructions for planting bare-root and b&b trees, on pages 34 and 35.)

Dig the first planting hole. Make it three times as wide but not quite as deep as the container. The tree will grow better if the top of its rootball sits 1 inch above the surrounding soil (3 inches above if your soil doesn't drain well). Leaving a plateau of firm soil for the tree to sit on, dig 2 inches deeper around the edges of the hole so that the roots can grow down into loose soil. Loosen the soil around the sides of the hole to help the roots penetrate laterally.

Remove the tree from its container. Try to slip it out by turning the container on its side and gently pulling it away from the plant. Don't yank on the trunk. Give the sides and base of the container a few sharp raps if the tree doesn't slide out easily. Cut away the container if necessary; slit it from rim to base in several places, being careful that you don't cut through any big roots.

Take a hard look at the rootball. If the roots are matted or circling the rootball, pry or cut them loose. Don't worry about breaking small roots on the edge of the rootball.

Set the tree into the planting hole, lifting it with one hand on the trunk, one under the rootball. Check that the top of the rootball is at least 1 inch above the soil surface. Fill in around the rootball with the soil you dug from the hole, working it firmly between the roots and lifting the tree if necessary to keep it above soil level. Mound soil around the exposed rootball to cover the roots. Press the soil firmly around the tree.

Make a watering moat by building a 4-inch-high dike of soil around the planting hole. Water the tree thoroughly. Plant the other tree.

Plant the lavenders in the same manner, but don't worry about making a plateau in the planting hole, and set the rootballs just ½ inch above soil level. Space the lavenders 3 feet apart at the edge of the tree canopy. (Because of competition from the tree roots and shade from the canopy, they won't grow well close to the trunk.)

Inexpensive
Easy
Location: Sun or shade; wind tolerated
Soil: Most kinds, including poor, dry ones
Tree hardiness: Zones 7–10

**Tools**
Measuring tape
Hose or watering can
Straight-edged spade
Trowel
Sharp knife

**Ingredients**
2 California bay trees (*Umbellularia californica*) or any tree common in natural landscape
English lavenders (*Lavandula angustifolia*), 1 per square yard

**Maintenance**
Water trees and lavender regularly until established, then only moderately
Shear lavenders immediately after bloom
Remove unwanted tree seedlings and suckers

# PINT-SIZED TREES

Many plants are treelike, which means only that they have a clear trunk and a crown of branches or stems. A succulent with those characteristics, such as a tree aloe, can pull your eye into a corner where its tall silhouette, dark as charcoal, moves across white walls, marking the hour like a sundial. Shrubs easily become trees with a little pruning in the early years, or they can be thinned in old age from dark thickets to multi-trunked mini trees with graceful lines. Vines that develop heavy branches, such as wisteria, can be trained to stand alone on a stem-turned-trunk and will grow for perhaps a century that way, blooming every spring with full-scale flowers.

You can peer into the tops of petite trees and look down into the forks of the branches where birds might nest and rain collect. The trunks gain the same character as those of old large trees, and the wind whistles just the same through the soft foliage in spring and takes on a dry rustle during fall. An extra-small tree even provides height and verticality to the garden if you keep the ground cover low beneath it. Choose a low ground cover with tiny leaves, and the tree soars over it like a giant. Add small rocks to further confuse the scale, and you can create a miniaturized landscape under the tree, a garden of the imagination.

Many trees can be kept small by growing them in containers. Select a large container. Protect the tree or bring it into a conservatory through the winter unless you live in a warm-winter climate.

# BLUE-TRUNKED CAMELLIAS

Camellia shrubs had grown into an almost impenetrable thicket along the side of the house, so the new owners, garden designers Shari and Richard Sullivan, pruned them up into trees. It was their young son Brendan's idea to paint the legs blue.

Each camellia is a distinct presence now, one stepping this way, another leaning that way. The glossy green foliage screens the neighbor's house and is studded for months with cup-sized blossoms. The flowers drop whole and perfect, nail polish red and pink, onto the pebbles and sand around the blue trunks.

As you stroll through, picking your way over the blossoms, pricks of light dart through the dense canopy and flicker in penny pieces over the fence, wall, path, and trunks. The sparkle is a teaser to the unobstructed sunlight streaming over the blue-walled patio at the end of the tunnel.

**HOW TO DO IT** ❮❮❮ These camellias (*Camellia japonica*) are 10 feet tall and probably about 20 years old. Although camellias are good choices for shady places, they are too large for narrow corridors, so don't plant a row of them in a cramped space; it will be years before they develop trunks like these. Buy vigorous, upright varieties and give them lots of space, as described below; perhaps even plant them in a grove. Or use the ideas in this project—the trunk-painting, pruning, and pebbles—to redesign any thicket of shrubs that has grown too large in your garden; see the directions at the end of the recipe for pruning an existing thicket.

Mark the locations for the camellias. Place them 6 feet apart and 4 feet from a path or fence if you want them to grow into trees. Water each plant in its container.

Dig the first planting hole. Make it three times as wide but not quite as deep as the container. The plant will grow better if the top of its rootball sits 1 inch above the surrounding soil (3 inches above if your soil doesn't drain well). Leaving a plateau of firm soil for the camellia to sit on, dig 2 inches deeper around the edges of the hole so that the roots can grow down into loose soil. Loosen the soil around the sides of the hole to help the roots penetrate laterally.

Remove the camellia from its container. Try to slip it out by turning the container on its side and gently pulling it away from the plant. Don't yank on the trunk. Give the sides and base of the container a few sharp raps if the plant doesn't slide out easily. Cut away the container if necessary; slit it from rim to base in several places, being careful that you don't cut through any big roots.

Set the camellia into the planting hole, lifting it with one hand on the trunk, one under the rootball. Check that the top of the rootball is at least 1 inch above the soil surface. Fill in around the rootball with the soil you dug from the hole, working it firmly between the roots and lifting the camellia if necessary to keep it above soil level. Mound soil around the exposed rootball to cover the roots. Press the soil firmly around the plant.

Make a watering moat by building a 4-inch-high dike of soil around the planting hole. Water the camellia thoroughly. Plant the others.

Spread the pebbles around the camellias. They tie the planting together, keep the roots cool, and suppress weeds. It's best not to garden under

---

Moderately inexpensive
Easy
Location: Light shade, sheltered
Soil: Rich, well drained, acid
Tree hardiness: Zones 8–9, maybe 7 if
    well sheltered

**Tools**
Measuring tape
Hose or watering can
Straight-edged spade
Trowel
Sharp knife
Pruning shears
Newspapers
Blue latex (water-based) paint
Bucket, for diluting paint
Paintbrush

**Ingredients**
Camellias (*Camellia japonica*), tall varieties
    proven hardy in your area, 1 per 6 feet
    of path edge
Pebbles, round, river-washed, blue or gray

**Maintenance**
Water camellias regularly until estab-
    lished, then moderately
Fertilize regularly with an acid plant food
    designed for camellias
To encourage tall growth, shorten lower
    branches after second year, in fall;
    remove these the following year
Reapply paint every year or two

camellias because they have shallow sensitive roots. Lay the pebbles 1 to 2 inches deep, being careful not to damage the trunks of the camellias.

After the second year, you can begin pruning the camellias into tree forms. In summer or fall, shorten the lowest branches, which will encourage the top growth. Be patient: don't shorten more than a few branches. The following year, remove the shortened branches back to the trunk and shorten a few higher branches. Repeat this procedure until the tops of the shrubs are as high as you want them.

Paint the trunks: Lay newspaper to protect the pebbles from splashes. Pour equal amounts of water and latex paint into a clean bucket, mix thoroughly, and paint from the tree canopy to ground level.

If you've inherited a thicket, prune all the lowest branches back to the trunk. Proceed slowly, looking for opportunities to create interesting trunk angles, multiple trunks, forked trunks. Thin the canopy very lightly, by pruning side branches back to main branches. Don't get carried away; the tops should look full and healthy.

# AGRICULTURAL TERRACES, WEEPING MULBERRIES

The view would drop away helter-skelter down the steep hillside but for these broad, zigzagging garden terraces. The bold patterns of color arrest the eye comfortably on the flat. Gray-white succulents dot fields of wire vine; pork and beans colonize dry lakes of broken slate. At the garden wall stand two weeping mulberry trees, sentinels between the miniaturized landscape of the terraces and the steep woods beyond.

From the house, you have a bird's-eye view into the tops of the mulberries. Smooth gray branches spume from the center and cascade in fountains of rich green foliage to the floor. In summer, when the terraces bake in the heat, each mulberry becomes a miniature shade pavilion covered in sweet black fruits.

# HOW TO DO IT ◄◄◄

These weeping mulberries (*Morus alba* 'Pendula') are 15 years old and approximately 6 feet tall. The trees stand in a field of wire vine, with patches of hen and chicks. A neighboring terrace, needing very little water, contains pork and beans and scattered slate. In other terraces grow more "crop" plants with miniature features, such as snow-in-summer (*Cerastium tomentosum*) and kleinias (*Senecio serpens* 'Chalksticks').

If you are making terraces from scratch, make them broad, and have them descend the hillside in irregular, strong shapes, like the ancient rice terraces in the Philippines and Bali. Leave the terrace edges bare of plants to show off the shapes.

Mark the locations for the trees. Place them on the lowest terrace, to camouflage the line where your miniaturized fields meet the edge of the garden or a different area of it. Place the trees 6 feet apart, at least 2 feet from the terrace edge.

Water each tree in its container. (If your trees are not in containers, see the instructions for planting bare-root and b&b trees, on pages 34 and 35.)

Dig the first planting hole. Make it three times as wide but not quite as deep as the container. The tree will grow better if the top of its rootball sits 1 inch above the surrounding soil (3 inches above if your soil doesn't drain well). Leaving a plateau of firm soil for the tree to sit on, dig 2 inches deeper around the edges of the hole so that the roots can grow down into loose soil. Loosen the soil around the sides of the hole to help the roots penetrate laterally.

Remove the tree from its container. Try to slip it out by turning the container on its side and gently pulling it away from the plant. Don't yank on the trunk. Give the sides and base of the container a few sharp raps if the tree doesn't slide out easily. Cut away the container if necessary; slit it from rim to base in several places, being careful that you don't cut through any big roots.

Take a hard look at the rootball. If the roots are matted or circling the rootball, pry or cut them loose. Don't worry about breaking small roots on the edge of the rootball.

Set the tree into the planting hole, lifting it with one hand on the trunk, one under the rootball. Check that the top of the rootball is at least 1 inch above the soil surface. Fill in around the rootball with the soil you dug from the hole, working it firmly between the roots and lifting the tree if necessary to keep it above soil level. Mound soil around the exposed rootball to cover the roots. Press the soil firmly around the tree.

Inexpensive
Moderately easy
Location: Full sun
Soil: Most kinds, including alkaline ones
Tree hardiness: Zones 5–9

## Tools

Measuring tape
Hose or watering can
Straight-edged spade
Trowel
Sharp knife
Hammer, or mallet
4 tree stakes, or two-by-twos, 7 feet long
Plastic tree ties, 4 pieces, each 4 feet long
White latex paint
Bucket, for diluting paint
Paintbrush

## Ingredients

2 weeping mulberry trees (*Morus alba* 'Pendula')
Hen and chicks (*Echeveria elegans*), 7 clumps of 5 plants each
Wire vine (*Muehlenbeckia* spp.), 36 per square yard
Slate, shattered pieces of different sizes
Pork and beans (*Sedum rubrotinctum*), 36 per square yard

## Maintenance

Water trees and plants regularly until established; continue to water wire vine and trees regularly if you want most rapid growth; hen and chicks and pork and beans require only a little summer watering once established
Remove stakes and ties in second year
Thin trees after several years, to keep trunks visible

Make a watering moat by building a 4-inch-high dike of soil around the planting hole. Water the tree thoroughly. Plant the second tree.

Stake each tree: Hammer one stake into the ground 1 foot from the trunk, and another on the other side of the tree, again 1 foot from the trunk. Tie the tree to each stake about 4 feet from the ground, using two lengths of flexible tree tie and leaving the ties on the loose side, so that the tree moves a little in the wind.

Plant seven irregular patches of hen and chicks across the terrace; space the individual plants 6 inches apart in the patches. Plant the rest of the terrace with wire vine, spaced 6 inches apart. Water the plants after planting.

In the adjoining terrace, scatter the slate in two streams across the terrace, perhaps mimicking the line that water might take flowing down the hillside. Cover the rest of the terrace with pork and beans, spaced 6 inches apart. Water the plantings.

For effect, as much as to prevent sunburn, whitewash the tree trunks before their first summer. Pour equal quantities of paint and water in a clean bucket, mix thoroughly, and brush the paint onto the trunks.

The tree branches will weep to the floor as the trees grow. Gradually thin the canopies after a few years if they become so dense that you can't see the trunks; remove the thickest branches, cutting right back to the top of the trunk, leaving no stubs.

# WISTERIA TREE WITH TULIPS

Every summer and winter for decades, someone has been out in the garden with pruners attending to this mighty vine-turned-tree. In summer, streamers of new stems spume from the knotty branches, spiraling clockwise through thin air, in the event there's something nearby to climb on. In winter, when the ground is crusty cold, the vine must be pruned more, into wood rather than soft stem, to ensure that all the wild vining energy is turned into spring blooms.

There's also regular, meticulous work to be done below the trees. The boxwood needs trimming on three sides twice a year to keep it neat. In fall, the bulbs go in, 36 per square yard.

The satisfaction is in handling the shiny papery chestnut sheaths on the tulip bulbs, setting the dumpy bases of the bulbs on the crumbling cold earth in holes you've made as geometric as a pegboard. And when the sun shines, the warmth releases a musty scent from the boxwood that proud skilled gardeners smelled centuries ago.

# HOW TO DO IT ◄◄◄

This double-flowered Japanese wisteria tree (*Wisteria floribunda* 'Plena') is about 6 feet tall and 50 to 60 years old. It is kept to this size by regular pruning. You might buy a vine already trained to tree form, or start with a young vine (budded or grafted or grown from a cutting, but not from seed) and train it up a stake yourself, as described below. Boxwood hedges surround the wisteria; tulips bloom beneath it in spring. Several very stout tree props hold up the heavy branches.

Mark the planting site for the tree; choose a prominent position where it can be viewed from all sides. Avoid windy sites if you are training it yourself.

Start establishing the tree form before planting a young vine. Earmark the largest, strongest stem as the future tree trunk, and prune all the others back to the base. Water the vine, now just a single stem, in its container.

Dig the planting hole. Make it three times as wide but not quite as deep as the container. The plant will grow better if the top of its rootball sits 1 inch above the surrounding soil (3 inches above if your soil doesn't drain well). Leaving a plateau of firm soil for the plant to sit on, dig 2 inches deeper around the edges of the hole so that the roots can grow down into loose soil. Loosen the soil around the sides of the hole to help the roots penetrate laterally.

Position the stake before planting the vine. Hammer it into the center of the plateau until it is very firm (the tip at least 1 to 2 feet below ground). Rebuild the plateau if it has crumbled, making it as firm as you can.

Remove the vine from its container. Try to slip it out by turning the container on its side and gently pulling it away from the plant. Don't yank on the stem. Give the sides and base of the container a few sharp raps if the vine doesn't slide out easily. Cut away the container if necessary; slit it from rim to base in several places, being careful that you don't cut through any big roots.

Take a hard look at the rootball. If the roots are matted or circling the rootball, pry or cut them loose. Don't worry about breaking small roots on the edge of the rootball.

Set the wisteria into the planting hole, lifting it with one hand on the stem, one under the rootball. Nestle it to within 2 inches of the stake, prying or washing away soil from the rootball as necessary. Check that the top of the rootball is at least 1 inch above the soil surface. Fill in around the rootball with the soil you dug from the hole, working it firmly between the roots and lifting the wisteria if necessary to keep it above soil level. Mound soil around the exposed rootball to cover the roots. Press the soil firmly around the plant.

Inexpensive
Moderately easy
Location: Full sun
Soil: Most well-drained kinds
Vine hardiness: Zones 6–8

**Tools**
Pruners
Hose or watering can
Straight-edged spade
Trowel
Hammer or mallet
1 stout tree stake, 8 feet tall
Sharp knife
Flexible plant ties

**Ingredients**
1 Japanese wisteria (*Wisteria floribunda* 'Plena'), young vine, or vine already trained into tree
Boxwood hedge (*Buxus* spp.) (optional), 4 plants per 1 yard of hedge
'Angelique' and 'Mount Tacoma' tulips, 12 of each per 1 yard of 2-foot-wide planting bed

**Maintenance**
Water vine regularly until it is established, then only moderately
Prune vine in August and December or January (see text)
Renew stake and plant ties as necessary; substitute tree props after a few years
Water tulips, unless it rains, every 5 days from the time leaves emerge through flowering
When tulip flowers fade, cut flower stems but let leaves die back before trimming
Clip boxwood (optional) once or twice a year

Make a watering moat by building a 4-inch-high dike of soil around the planting hole. Water the wisteria thoroughly.

After planting, secure the vine to the stake in several places with flexible plant ties. As the vine grows (once it gets started, it will grow rapidly), secure the new growth to the stake with more ties. When the vine reaches 6 feet, pinch out the tip of it to force it to produce branches.

When the branches grow, select three, and shorten them by one third to make them stouter. Remove any other branches. You now have the framework of the tree.

In August each year, leave a few of the side shoots that grow from the branches to form side branches. Cut back the rest to stubs, 6 to 9 inches long. Watch for new buds on the trunk of the vine, below the branches, and rub these off before shoots form, so the trunk remains clear. Remove any suckers that grow from the base of the vine.

In December or January each year, shorten the stubs you made in August to 3 or 4 inches. These are the flowering spurs, and you want lots of them. Also shorten the main branches and the new side branches, by one third, to keep them stout.

When the branches are about 4 feet long, stop them there, by removing new growth back to 6 inches in August, to form flowering spurs.

Remove the stake after a few years. Support the branches with tree props.

Make a boxwood hedge (optional): Plant the boxwood plants in the same manner as the vine, but don't worry about making a plateau in the planting hole, and set the rootballs just ½ inch above soil level. Space them 9 inches apart around a 2-foot-wide planting bed, the vine at the center of the bed.

Plant the tulips in October (December in warm-winter climates). For a formal look, mark out equidistant holes on a diagonal grid, 6 inches between holes in all directions. Make the holes 6 inches deep. Place the tulip bulbs with their pointy tips up, cover them with soil, firm the soil, and water generously. Until the rainy season starts, water weekly.

# BIRCH-GIRL AT A CROSSROADS

This unnaturally contorted, skinny, white-trunked birch with flimsy shivering skirts is planted in a place where it can be stared at. Three paths, from the directions of the three silver balls in its crown, meet here at a crossroads. It marks such an important, much-traveled place, visible from almost every part of this small urban garden, that the tree has to have plenty of chutzpah, like an old oak on a village green.

Passing by, then back again later, you can touch it if you'd like to. Thin sheets of bark curl off the trunk, especially on the insides of the curves. The leaves swish about, hiding and revealing glimpses of what's underneath.

In spring, fans of soft green leaves burst from the weeping branches; in fall they turn honey yellow; and in winter the tree is entirely nude, except for a crop of dark small cones—and the silver balls that record all these moments as well as your enchanted gazing.

# HOW TO DO IT ⋘

This Young's weeping birch (*Betula pendula* 'Youngii') is about 10 years old and fully grown; it reached its mature height 5 years ago. The branches have been thinned, to reveal the trunk. The tree was purchased already trained into a spiral, from a tree nursery at a gardening show. You could try to special-order a spiral-trained one from a nursery; or start with a very young tree, a whip, and train it around a stake yourself, as described below.

Mark the planting site; place the tree in a prominent position, where paths meet, at the house entrance, or at the destination of a walk. Avoid windy sites if you are training the tree yourself.

Water the tree (whether you are starting with a whip or an already-trained tree) in its container. (If your tree is not in a container, see the instructions for planting bare-root and b&b trees, on pages 34 and 35.)

Dig the planting hole. Make it three times as wide but not quite as deep as the container. The tree will grow better if the top of its rootball sits 1 inch above the surrounding soil (3 inches above if your soil doesn't drain well). Leaving a plateau of firm soil for the tree to sit on, dig 2 inches deeper around the edges of the hole so that the roots can grow down into loose soil. Loosen the soil around the sides of the hole to help the roots penetrate laterally.

If you are training the tree from a whip, position the tree stake. Hammer it into the center of the plateau until it is very firm (the tip at least 1 to 2 feet below ground). Rebuild the plateau if it has crumbled, making it as firm as you can.

Remove the tree from its container. Try to slip it out by turning the container on its side and gently pulling it away from the plant. Don't yank on the trunk. Give the sides and base of the container a few sharp raps if the tree doesn't slide out easily. Cut away the container if necessary; slit it from rim to base in several places, being careful that you don't cut through any big roots.

Take a hard look at the rootball. If the roots are matted or circling the rootball, pry or cut them loose. Don't worry about breaking small roots on the edge of the rootball.

Set the tree into the planting hole, lifting it with one hand on the trunk, one under the rootball. Nestle it to within 2 inches of the stake, if you are planting a whip for training, prying or washing away soil from the rootball as necessary. Check that the top of the rootball is at least 1 inch above the soil

Inexpensive
Easy
Location: Full sun or light shade; dry hot conditions not tolerated
Soil: Most kinds, except dry ones
Tree hardiness: Zones 3–7

### Tools
Hose or watering can
Straight-edged spade
Trowel
Hammer or mallet
1 tree stake, or two-by-two, 7 feet long
Sharp knife
Flexible tree ties

### Ingredients
1 Young's weeping birch (*Betula pendula* 'Youngii'), a whip, to train, or an already-trained tree

### Maintenance
Water tree regularly; it is prone to serious pests and diseases if watered insufficiently
Watch for signs of pests and diseases; seek analysis and treatment quickly
In summer or fall, prune low branches and thin canopy as necessary (see text)

surface. Fill in around the rootball with the soil you dug from the hole, working it firmly between the roots and lifting the tree if necessary to keep it above soil level. Mound soil around the exposed rootball to cover the roots. Press the soil firmly around the tree.

Make a watering moat by building a 4-inch-high dike of soil around the planting hole. Water the tree thoroughly.

If you are training the tree from a whip: After planting, twist the whip around the stake, one twist every 2 feet. Secure the whip to the stake in several places with tree ties, looping the ties in a figure eight so that the whip beats against the tie, not the stake, in windy weather. As the tree grows, keep twisting the trunk around the stake. After the second year, in summer or fall, shorten any branches low on the trunk and remove them the following year. When the tree reaches the top of the stake, let it weep.

As the tree matures, thin the crown as necessary to keep the trunk visible, by removing side branches back to main branches or a main branch back to the trunk. To emphasize the swing in the shape of the tree, select for pruning first those branches that are on the inside of the curves.

# SOURCES OF TREES

*Your local nursery probably stocks a selection of trees suited to local soils and climate. The nurseries listed here are mail-order sources for trees; some are also open to the public.*

**Carroll Gardens**
444 East Main Street
Westminster, MD 21157
Tel: (800) 638-6334
Fax: (410) 857-4112
*Catalog $3. Nursery is open to public.*

**Fairweather Gardens**
P. O. Box 330
Greenwich, NJ 08323
Tel: (609) 451-6261
Fax: (609) 451-0303
*Catalog $3. No shipments to the western states.*

**Forestfarm**
Ray and Peg Prag
990 Tetherow Road
Williams, OR 97544-9599
Tel: (541) 846-7269
Fax: (541) 846-6963
e-mail: forestfarm@aonepro.net
www.forestfarm.com
*Catalog $4. Nursery is open to public.*

**Gossler Farms Nursery**
1200 Weaver Road
Springfield, OR 97478
Tel: (541) 746-3922
Fax: (541) 744-7924
*Catalog $2. Nursery is open to public by appointment; please call.*

**Heronswood Nursery**
7530 NE 288th Street
Kingston, WA 98346-9502
Tel: (360) 297-4172
Fax: (360) 297-8321
e-mail: heronswood@silverlink.net
www.heronswood.com
*Catalog $5. Nursery is open to public by appointment; please call.*

**Louisiana Nursery**
5853 Highway 182
Opelousas, LA 70570
Tel: (318) 948-3696
Fax: (318) 942-6404
*Tree catalog $6. Nursery is open to public, but please call first.*

**Musser Forests, Inc.**
P.O. Box 340, Route 119 North
Indiana, PA 15701-0340
Tel: (800) 643-8319
Fax: (724) 465-9893
e-mail: info@musserforests.com
www.musserforests.com
*Free spring and fall catalogs. Garden center, (724) 465-5684, is open to public.*

**Roslyn Nursery**
211 Burrs Lane
Dix Hills, NY 11746
Tel: (516) 643-9347
Fax: (516) 427-0894
e-mail: roslyn@concentric.net
www.cris.com/~Roslyn/
*Catalog $3. Nursery is open to public.*

**Woodlanders**
1128 Colleton Avenue
Aiken, SC 29801
Tel: (803) 648-7522
Fax: (803) 648-7522
e-mail: woodlanders@scescape.net
*Catalog $2. Nursery is open to public by appointment; please call.*

# BIBLIOGRAPHY

*The following books have inspired and informed my writing on trees:*

Alexander, Christopher, Sara Ishikawa, and Murray Silverstein. *A Pattern Language.* New York: Oxford University Press, 1977.

Bender, Steve, ed. *Southern Living Garden Book.* Birmingham, Alabama: Oxmoor House, 1998.

Calvino, Italo. *The Baron in the Trees.* San Diego: Harcourt Brace and Company, 1977.

Church, Thomas D., Grace Hall, and Michael Laurie. *Gardens Are for People.* Berkeley and Los Angeles: University of California Press, 1995.

Coombes, Allen J. *Trees: The Visual Guide to More Than 500 Species of Trees from around the World.* New York: DK Publishing, 1992.

Crowe, Sylvia. *Garden Design.* Wappingers Falls, New York: Antique Collectors' Club, 1994.

Dirr, Michael A. *Manual of Woody Landscape Plants: Their Identification, Ornamental Characteristics, Culture, Propagation and Uses.* Champaign, Illinois: Stipes Publishing Company, 1990.

Fowles, John. *The Tree.* Photographs by William Neill. Berkeley, California: Nature Company, 1994.

Garden Club of America. *Plants That Merit Attention,* edited by Janet M. Poor. Volume 1: *Trees.* Portland, Oregon: Timber Press, 1984.

Hessayon, D. G. *The Tree and Shrub Expert.* New York: Expert Books, 1993.

Jacobson, Arthur Lee. *North American Landscape Trees.* Berkeley, California: Ten Speed Press, 1996.

Johnson, Hugh. *The Principles of Gardening.* New York: Simon and Schuster, 1984.

Kourik, Robert. *Bob's Honest-to-Goodness Newsletter* 1, no. 3 (fall 1995). P.O. Box 1841, Santa Rosa, CA 95402.

Page, Russell. *The Education of a Gardener.* New York: HarperCollins Publishers, 1994.

Sitwell, Sir George. *On the Making of Gardens.* New York: Scribners Sons, 1951. (Out of print.)

*Sunset National Garden Book.* Menlo Park, California: Sunset Books, 1997.

*Sunset Western Garden Book.* Menlo Park, California: Sunset Publishing, 1995.

*Taylor's Guide to Trees.* Boston: Houghton Mifflin, 1987.

*Trees: A Gardener's Guide.* Brooklyn, New York: Brooklyn Botanic Garden, 1992.

*Trees and Shrubs.* Menlo Park, California: Sunset Publishing, 1993.

# ACKNOWLEDGMENTS

I'm especially grateful to the many landscape architects, garden designers, and professional gardeners who shared their enthusiasms about tree gardens with me, especially Dan Borroff, Jack Chandler, Marcia Donahue, Don Ellis, Isabelle Greene, Rich Haag, Ron Herman, Sharon Osmond, Robin Parer, Michael Schultz, Richard Sullivan and Shari Bashin-Sullivan, Chris Tebbutt and Stephanie Kotin, and David Yakish.

Matt and I are also greatly indebted to all those who opened their gardens to us for this book. Thank you for your generosity—we were inspired by it and the many hours we spent studying your beautiful trees.

Many thanks to Michael Alliger, a teacher and aesthetic pruner of ornamental trees, from Sebastopol, California, for reviewing the technical sections of the manuscript. And to Jane Staw for reading much of the manuscript for clarity and grace.

The team at Chronicle Books put the book together smoothly and considerately. Particular thanks to our editor, Leslie Jonath, managing editor Dean E. Burrell, Jr., copy editor and dear friend Zipporah Collins, and designer David Bullen.

Finally, thanks to our families and friends, especially Margarita Kloss, Carol Henderson, Mimi Luebbermann, Nancy Warner, Sean Cotter, Mary Rodocker, Bill Klein, and Larry Weiss, for encouragement and humor.

# GARDEN CREDITS

*Gardens and garden owners are listed in roman type; the landscape architect or designer in italics.*
BellaMadrona, near Portland, Oregon: pages 1, 9, 56, 57, 84 (*Ceremonial Gateway* by Michael S. Schultz), 94. Bloedel Reserve, Bainbridge Island, Washington: pages 2, 3, 16 (bottom), 19, 22 (bottom), 26, 29, 36 (bottom), 39, 86, 88. *Marcia Donahue:* pages 4 (steel sculptures by Mark Bulwinkle), 18, 77, 79. *Stephanie Kotin and Christopher Tebbutt, Land & Place:* page 6. *Isabelle Greene,* Santa Barbara: pages 11, 13, 24 (bottom), 38 (top), 53, 67, 69, 98, 103. Jack Chandler, *Jack Chandler & Associates:* pages 12 (sculpture by Jack Chandler), 17 (top), 58. *Sharon Osmond:* pages 14, 15, 109. Eileen and Alex Tanfani, *David Yakish, gardenmakers:* pages 16 (top), 50, 51, 52, 80, 82. Wendy and Ron Klages, *Dan Borroff Landscape:* pages 20 (top), 23 (bottom), 28 (bottom), 64, 66. Filoli Gardens: page 20 (bottom). Gay Edelson, *Richard and Shari Sullivan, Enchanting Planting:* pages 21 (top), 37. Lavina and Glenn Stinson, *Ron Herman, ASLA:* pages 24 (top), 40. Jeff and Vivi Mitchell, Beija-flor Inn, Philo, Calif., *Stephanie Kotin and Christopher Tebbutt, Land & Place:* pages 25, 42, 48, 49, 73, 75. Scurlock residence, *Nancy Hammer Landscape Design:* pages 28 (top), 31. Mimi Luebbermann: page 30. Ron and Pamela Harrison, *Stephanie Kotin and Christopher Tebbutt, Land & Place:* page 32. Robin Parer: page 34 (sculpture by Simple). Residence on American Lake, Lakewood, Washington, *Dan Borroff Landscape:* page 41. Virginia and Arnie Israelit, *Michael S. Schultz:* pages 44, 45, 70, 72. Jack and Marilyn Jenkins-Stark, *Richard and Shari Sullivan, Enchanting Planting:* pages 46, 47. The Elizabeth F. Gamble Garden Center, 1431 Waverley Street, Palo Alto, Calif.: pages 61, 63, 106, 108. Real Goods Solar Living Center, Hopland, Calif., *Stephanie Kotin and Christopher Tebbutt, Land & Place:* pages 89, 90, 91. Wilbur and Linda Kukes, *Richard Haag, FASLA, RAAR:* page 92 (*Olla Maiden* by Kit Schweitzer). Long Meadow Ranch, *Jack Chandler & Associates:* pages 96 (*Long Meadow* sculpture by Jack Chandler), 97. *Richard and Shari Sullivan, Enchanting Planting:* page 100.

# INDEX

memorial
laundry
Draw - 1hr.
sunbathe - 1hr
(W) Sale Barber - 1hr
Gym Tu 1hr
B. garden - 1hr
Check Bass pro, library, Bricktown   2 hr
Tues - gym